P9-EEJ-711

Also by John Wain

Poetry

A Word Carved on a Sill
Weep Before God
Wildtrack
Letters to Five Artists

Fiction

Hurry on Down
Living in the Present
The Contenders
A Travelling Woman
Nuncle and Other Stories
Strike the Father Dead
The Young Visitors
Death of the Hind Legs and Other Stories
The Smaller Sky
A Winter in the Hills
The Life Guard

Autobiography

Sprightly Running

Criticism

Preliminary Essays
Essays on Literature and Ideas
The Living World of Shakespeare

A HOUSE FOR THE TRUTH

Critical Essays

John Wain

The Viking Press | New York

Published in 1973 by The Viking Press, Inc.
625 Madison Avenue, New York, N.Y. 10022
SBN 670-38015-6
Library of Congress catalog card number: 72-9411
Printed in U.S.A.

CONTENTS

ACKNOWLEDGEMENTS

'A Salute to the Makers', 'Radio Till Now', 'Dr Johnson's Poetry' and ' "To write for my own race" : Notes on the Fiction of Flann O'Brien' (in a shorter form; the essay printed in this book includes new material published here for the first time) first appeared in *Encounter.*

'The Vanishing Critic' first appeared in the *Listener*; 'Orwell in the Thirties' in *The World of George Orwell* edited by Miriam Gross and published by Weidenfeld & Nicolson, 1971; 'The meaning of *Dr Zhivago*' and 'The New Puritanism, the New Academism, the New, The New . . .' in the *Critical Quarterly*; 'Thinking Russian' in the *Malahat Review*, Victoria, British Columbia.

I have seen the meteors of fashion rise and fall, without any attempt to add a moment to their duration.

SAMUEL JOHNSON, *Rambler 208*

Introduction

THREE of these essays deal with prose fiction, though in one case the writer concerned was for fifty years known primarily as a poet, and his one great novel shows a constant, instinctive effort to apply to fiction what he had learnt in poetry. And in another case the novelist concerned is never far from a wild poetry, from the simultaneous exploration of different levels and the 'black humour' of the Surrealists. A fourth essay deals with the poetry of a man primarily remembered as a prose-writer and a talker.

My subjects, then, are poetry and fiction, and at the moments when I observe them they seem always to be merging into each other. The only unmixed writer here, a straight prosaist with not very much poetry in his composition, is George Orwell. And my interest in Orwell is primarily a moral interest. He was an admirably clear and forthright craftsman rather than a great artist; it is true of him, as it is not true of, for instance, Shakespeare or Michelangelo, that one's concern is with the man behind the work, rather than with the work itself. For this reason, my essay on Orwell is more biographical, more concerned to portray a certain man in a certain situation, than any of the others. But this, too, has links elsewhere in the book. If Orwell is a moral hero to me, a hero in the Carlylean sense, so are Johnson and Pasternak, though in these pages I discuss them primarily as artists.

If prose merges with verse and art merges with personality and life-style, it follows that one of the chief problems of criticism is to set boundaries. How much can the critic legitimately undertake? What can be picked up in the grab of a critical essay? Are there some subjects which are genuinely outside the legitimate concern of the critic? And so I find myself writing an essay on the essential unity of imaginative writing, the artificiality of splitting it into 'poetry' and 'fiction'. (Perhaps the real division is between poetry-and-criticism on the one hand, and drama on the other. I do not know.)

It is more than ever important to recognize and cherish the unity of imaginative writing at a time when such writing is under attack. And so the concluding essay tries to take stock of the attack.

This book, then, is offered as something more than a collection of fragments that have taken my fancy from the output of the last eight years. It is offered as a *book*, with unity of theme and recurring preoccupations. And the title? It comes from an essay by the detective-story writer, Raymond Chandler. I cannot now find the passage—it was in a book I was idly leafing through in someone else's house—but I remember that Chandler dismissed the notion that a critic is essentially a purveyor of fine phrases, sensitive cadences, witty aphorisms: 'the great critic', wrote this seasoned practitioner of fiction, 'builds a house for the truth'.

The phrase stuck in my mind, or, at any rate, what I thought was the phrase. It has since been pointed out to me that what Chandler wrote was 'a *home* for the truth'. Evidently I had unconsciously altered it, while it marinated in my memory, to a form of words more to my liking. But misquotation is always revealing one way or the other, and I don't propose to change it back now. I have taken it for the title of this book, not because I think myself 'a great critic' but because, in this throw-away age, the notion of building something as solid as a house seems to me true and salutary. Our current purveyors of pop art and instant kulch would agree that art communicates truth, whatever interpretation they would give to the word; but they would see it as truth flashed on a screen, or uttered over a public-address system; today's truth, to be replaced after one night by tomorrow's truth, and therefore not in need of any solid habitat. That is the dominant contemporary attitude to art; I dissent from it; this book is the fruit of my dissent. I dedicate it to the longest-serving editor of the magazine that has done most to keep serious issues before us: and to all unblown minds.

J.W.

January 1972

PART ONE

The Framework

A Salute to the Makers

MOST people would agree that the 'forms' of literature have no importance in themselves, that they are simply conveniences. A writer, essentially considered, is an imaginative person who seeks to convey his imaginative vision to his fellow-men by means of words, just as if he were a painter he would try to convey it in terms of colour and shape, or if a musician in terms of sounds. His medium is the dictionary, especially that great dictionary which is forever writing itself on the lips of a nation in speech. Whether he chops his lines up into lengths and calls the result 'poetry', or writes long narratives, or short narratives, or breaks up his stories into dialogue and distributes them among a company of actors to play on a stage—these are interesting decisions, but secondary ones.

Essentially, as I say, this is so. The trouble is that these conveniences, these 'forms', are *so* convenient that there is a constant and largely unnoticed pressure on us to over-rate them. If somebody decides to give a course of lectures on 'the novel', for instance, and begins to read and make notes and shape his material, he must necessarily group his chosen writers in an artificial relationship with one another, and deny them their natural relationship with other writers; he must cut them out of the herd, away from the poets and playwrights with whom they would normally co-exist, and corral them together as 'novelists' because they chose a particular form. And if any of these novelists happens to have made the attempt to convey his imaginative vision also in poetry, as Hardy did or as Meredith did or as Lawrence did or as I do, then he must expect to have the whole poetic side of his work lopped off and thrown into an antiseptic dustbin, to be dissected when somebody gets round to a study of 'poetry'—that somebody in turn, of course, ignoring prose fiction as 'not within the scope of this study' or some other churchwardenly formula for the covering-up of timidity and incompetence. If a poet happens to be a dramatist, as Eliot was, then the critics of drama will discuss his plays at length and mention his poetry only incidentally, if at all; and *vice versa*. This situation is not only bad for critics, making them even more lazy and unadventurous than nature made them to begin with; it is bad for writers as well, because for centuries every Western writer has grown up with the idea that the various literary forms are separated by tall hedges and that to break down one of those hedges—let alone break down two or three of them!—is an act of effrontery only to be justified by transcendent genius.

In the end one begins to think that it would be better if the conventional divisions between literary forms could be brainwashed out of us, if we could somehow wake up one morning knowing that there was imaginative writing but not knowing about Poetry, the Novel, Drama. Think of the bad criticism it would rid us of! I remember, when Dylan Thomas died, an obituary summing-up by a distinguished lady poet, who praised his poems and added rather sniffily that he had a useful gift for writing comic prose that must have been handy for pot-boiling —thus at one stroke blocking the natural avenue between Thomas's poems and the marvellous stories about growing up in *Portrait of the Artist as a Young Dog*, which are the natural accompaniment of his poems and obviously come from the same sensibility. To this lady poet, the fact that the stories were in prose automatically put them one step below the poems, because verse is Higher than prose, and the fact that they contained jokes bumped them down another two or three steps, because poetry is too Lofty to have any dealings with humour. Anyone who followed this line of approach would be bound to miss a great deal in Dylan Thomas's poetry, which uses the same rich playfulness of language as the stories, and is haunted by the same spirit of wild comedy: those generous explosions of metaphor burst out from some source of tragic exuberance that is never far from laughter.

No doubt I seem to be labouring the obvious, but I have been reading some books on poetry, and it has driven me to the conclusion that most of the really suffocating nonsense would disappear from the literary scene if the whole category of 'poetry' could somehow be dis-invented, if from now on no one called himself a poet, if there were no Poetry Fellowships or Poetry Awards or Poetry Evenings, if all writers were just called writers —or, if this did not differentiate the imaginative writer sufficiently from the authors of books on *Whither Liberalism?* or *How to Fiddle the Income Tax*, let the imaginative writer be called a 'maker' as he once was in Scotland. 'Maker' is of course the literal translation of ποιητής, poet, and as recently as the sixteenth century it was usual to apply the word 'poet' to any writer who showed imaginative vision; the Renaissance 'defences of poetry' against Puritan attack are not defences of *verse*, but of imagination, invention, symbolism, everything that is not a mere transcript of factual reality.

I admit that this Act of Oblivion would be attended by certain inconveniences. But these inconveniences would only affect bureaucrats of the arts, the kind of people who run the official 'poetry world'; and I am sure their ingenuity would be equal to the task of coping with any administrative problems that arose. For writers, and readers, the dis-invention of poetry would be marvellously liberating. It would put an end to all the various kinds of cant whose tendency is to single out the poet and make him feel that he is altogether different from other makers. It would be the end of a mystique, and a very bad and unhelpful mystique it has been. Who does not know the complacent egotist who, having got into print with a few slabs of incoherent maundering, considers it axiomatic that he is the natural superior of Harold Pinter or William Golding?

More important still, it would be the recognition of an existing situation. The breaking-down of barriers between the various literary forms has already happened, *de facto*, and might as well be admitted *de jure*. A hundred years ago, there was a general social expectation about the nature of poetry. If you opened a book of poetry, you saw that the lines were arranged metrically, and this prepared you for a suppler language and a more audacious use of metaphor. There was an unspoken compact between writer and reader: 'This is poetry. Don't expect the kind of thing you are used to in prose.' And the prose-writer, also, observed this gentleman's agreement. It was expected that prose should approximate to the language of normal discourse, and on the whole this expectation was fulfilled. Even Dickens, who was more of a poet than most of the verse-poets of his day, managed to stop short of the kind of prose-poetry that was to be written in France only a little later, by Lautréamont and Rimbaud.

This left the poet a clear field in which to be Lofty and also, if necessary, to be Difficult. Where the prose-writer had agreed to 'show his working', the poet could make unexplained jumps, and be allusive, and mysterious, in the knowledge that his public would take trouble to fathom out his meaning, and, if they did not succeed in fathoming it out, would keep that embarrassing fact to themselves. To some extent, the entire society said to all poets what Matthew Arnold had said to Shakespeare: 'Others abide our question: thou art free.' The poet was privileged, the prose-writer was not.

This situation has now completely disappeared. As all imaginative literature is more and more driven into a corner, the distinction between one maker and another becomes less and less important. Back in the 1950s, I remember noticing that Beckett's *Waiting for Godot* seemed more like poetry than most of the verse-plays which were, at that time, still enjoying a vogue. And the tendency has continued. With the disappearance of a mass public for the novel (the kind of writer who used to write mass-circulation novels now writes television sagas), the serious, 'literary' novel is now read by very much the same kind of person who reads poetry. Meanwhile the public for poetry itself has changed. The oral culture has brought the notion of 'poetry', if not always the thing itself, to a public completely different from the one that traditionally respected it; and, if present tendencies continue, will end by driving the traditional public away altogether.

These thoughts have been vaguely present to my mind for some time, but they have been brought to the surface by reading three new books about poetry, two of them first-rate and the third patchy. The first-rate ones are Michael Hamburger's *The Truth of Poetry* and Jerzy Peterkiewicz's *The Other Side of Silence*; the patchy one is *The Survival of Poetry*, edited by Martin Dodsworth, one of those worthy collections by 'several hands' that grow out of a series of public lectures. Such collections inevitably include a few duds, but with any luck they have some good things as well; there is, in this one, a first-rate critical essay (Barbara Hardy on Sylvia Plath) and several pieces which could, at any rate, serve as useful introductions. The fatuities, however, outweigh the good things, and it is probably true that books like this, which obtrude a screen of trend-talk between the reader and the poets, are best left alone.

It was Mr Hamburger's book that gave me most furiously to think, not only because of its high level of thoughtfulness and sensibility, but because it is so disturbingly informative. To be told about poet after poet, from country after country, to be shown examples of their work, to be introduced to their theories about poetry, and their views of the universe, and their personal circumstances, and the titles of their books, and the kind of thing they said in their letters, is to be (as another contemporary poet has put it) 'bombed with information'. Because Mr Hamburger knows so much about poetry, in so many languages, and has thought about it so deeply, and is such a good poet himself, and explains it so clearly without minimising the difficulties—because of these things, his book is truly frightening: I mean it makes me want to get up from my chair and run away. For what his book really demonstrates, as he knows perfectly well, is the sheer *chaos* of modern poetry, the lack of agreement about anything at all. Poetry is impersonal, so that the better the poet is, 'the more completely separate in him will be the man who suffers and the mind which creates' (T. S. Eliot); from another point of view, 'one of the great criticisms of poets of the past is that they said one thing and did another' (Philip Larkin). Chance, the random sweeping-together of material, is an important poetic principle because it counters the willed and the deliberate, which make art unreal (Jean Arp); on the contrary, a poem is 'a kind of machine for producing the poetic state of mind by means of words' (Paul Valéry). Yeats comes in somewhere between Eliot and Larkin with his doctrine of 'the mask', the notion that the way to achieve great poetry is to meditate on an imaginary being who is the exact opposite of oneself, and thus set up a creative tension between what all too obviously is and what might have been if you had been born an entirely different person. Somewhere between Arp and Valéry stands Jorge Guillén with his belief that the essential *haecceitas* of everything is embodied in the name we give to it, so that a noun like 'Rose' enshrines our memory of past roses and our anticipation of those we shall see in the future. Other poets have tried to strip away the coating of language and come directly at experience: a doctrine like Guillén's would make language, in its primary role of the naming of objects, the most direct avenue to experience. The ideal poetic state is purely instinctual, emptied of opinions, reduced to a simplicity that is almost pre-conscious (Gottfried Benn); no, it is an acceptance of normality and responsibility, a consciousness that includes everything that the ordinary man worries about (Franco Fortini). Poetry, to be effective, must purge itself of everything that smacks of invention and originality; its metaphors and similes must operate at the level of ordinary prose usage, that is to say below the point at which they are felt as metaphors and similes at all (Cesar Vallejo); no, answers Wallace Stevens, poetry must shimmer with analogies, it must thrive on correspondences which only the poet has perceived, because 'Poetry is a satisfying of the desire for resemblance'. Poetry is essentially an exploration, a groping into the dark of the poet's mind for meanings that only the act of creation will reveal (Dylan Thomas); no, its business is to tell its readers 'something they know and hadn't thought of saying' (Robert Frost). There seems no point in going on; the great strength of this book, and also what makes it unsettling, is that it demonstrates how little the poets of the modern world, with all the force of their art and the logic of their persuasion, have been able to convince one another. 'Each thing meets/In mere oppugnancy.'

If Mr Hamburger's book opens a window on to chaos, Mr Peterkiewicz also intensifies one's sense of the difficulties of the poet, but in a different way. He is concerned less with the sheer Babel of theory and practice than with the fundamental problems inherent in poetry as a means of perception. Where Mr Hamburger is exoteric, Mr Peterkiewicz by comparison is esoteric. He meditates intensely, and rather sombrely, on that side of the poet's experience which links him with the mystic and the visionary. Like Mr Hamburger, he refers to a wide range of examples, from many literatures; but, essentially, his main exhibits are rather few. He is really interested primarily in a handful of major visionary-poets whose spiritual biographies bring up in an acute form the question: how far towards the truth will poetry, in the end, carry us?

I found this book very fruitful, a tremendous stimulus towards meditation on the ultimates of poetry, and I am grateful for it. For this reason I shall pass lightly over what might otherwise be my doubts and reservations. Considered purely as a critical study, *The Other Side of Silence* is not quite satisfactory. Its scope is partial, and it consistently employs language that suggests that its scope is general. 'The poet' is habitually used in contexts where some such phrase as 'certain kinds of poet in certain situations' would have been more prudent. Further, in spite of a chapter called 'The Failure of Mystical Verse', Mr Peterkiewicz obviously has a large element of the mystical in his own imaginative composition, and assumes (mistakenly, in my opinion) that this is the rule rather than the exception, so that he can write:

> In his adoration of nature, the poet finds an obstacle: the obstacle is of the same kind as in any pantheistic concept of God. If deity is so widely and diversely represented in things, why should we feel the mystical thirst for the void, that is for the absence of natural phenomena?

It seems to me highly doubtful that Shakespeare, for instance, ever felt 'the mystical thirst for the void', or that such a thirst is necessarily a part of the experience of an artist, even an artist of the greatest intensity and widest range. But one learns, in reading this quite exceptional book, to allow for the steady pressure of Mr Peterkiewicz's interest in mystical experience, and to adjust the compass a few degrees accordingly. It hardly matters, because the luminous, concentrated atmosphere of his argument causes one to see everything in a slightly different perspective anyway.

Mr Peterkiewicz is interested in the poet at the point of crisis, the moment when he becomes dissatisfied with poetry. On his very first page, after instancing Rimbaud and St John of the Cross (the first of whom was stopped short by this crisis, while the second managed to struggle through it), he goes so far as to say that the 'profound dissatisfaction with poetry', perceptible in these poets, 'seems to be inherent in the best of poetry'. That 'seems', which indicates a willingness to admit doubt, pretty soon becomes 'is', and we learn to recognize in Mr Peterkiewicz one of those imaginative writers to whom the mystical life is very real, whose inward gaze is fixed on

A certain marvellous thing
None but the living mock.

Of course we often meet with this predisposition among artists, and not necessarily those whose *persona* is most spiritual and other-worldly; Roy Campbell was a man of action and a soldier, yet his widow has put it on record that 'his first great enthusiasm was for Rimbaud and his last for St John of the Cross'. These two writers, naturally, are central to Mr Peterkiewicz's book. Other poets come in more or less incidentally, and sometimes with the air of being in unexpected company. (Hopkins, for instance, doesn't really fit in next to his contemporary Norwid, though he can be made to appear to do so.)

Mr Peterkiewicz's book cannot be said to have a 'thesis', but it has a hub round which the various meditations revolve, and the hub is this. Poets drive towards truth in the chariot of language. But sooner or later the horses drop dead or a wheel comes off, and they have to get down and walk. For most of them, this is the end of their dream of arriving at the truth; but in one or two cases the poet manages to get as far as an ideal sanctuary in which truth is perceived so directly that it hardly matters any longer whether he speaks or remains silent, because those of us who have not made this journey will hardly understand him in any case. St John of the Cross is the hero of the book, because his poetry records a state of joyful reconciliation in which negatives become positives: having cast off all earthly attachments, the saint achieves an even more intense and consuming form of love, the love of the pure spirit of God which lies beyond all material experiences and is their foundation.

Personally, being closed in 'the muddy vesture of decay', I find all this part of Mr Peterkiewicz's book unconvincing. But that is because all my most profound experiences, from making love to watching a sunset, have come to me through the medium of concrete, measurable realities. (I don't say that the experiences themselves have been concrete and measurable; I say that the medium was.) All those high ecstatic states which are to be experienced in the stratosphere, above the perception of physical reality, are unknown to me and I suppose always will be unknown, which is why even a minor earth-inhabiting poet means more to me than a high mystical poet; when the chips are down, I would rather read Herrick than St John of the Cross, though I can see he is nothing like so important. To Mr Peterkiewicz, it is St John first, the rest nowhere; he is the only finisher, because when poetry failed him and silence closed in, he was able to go on and make poetry out of the transcendent paradox of total indifference towards the world in which poetry is rooted. In Mr Peterkiewicz's terms, his poetry comes to us from 'the other side of silence'. But even as he describes this miracle, Mr Peterkiewicz seems half unable to believe that it really happened. Contemplating the prose treatises which St John provided as commentaries on his mystical poems, he writes:

One wonders how much his systematic interpretations detach the poems from the aura of the other side, while they succeed in making them clear to us on this side. Was St John dissatisfied with poetry? The way in which his prose developed from three lyrical records of ecstasy seems to imply that. A poet's intelligence is present in his mystical tracts but it is well harnessed to pure discourse.

Even St John, it seems, has to be shown as 'dissatisfied with poetry', the real reason being that Mr Peterkiewicz has made up his mind in advance that all the best poets are. Similarly Boris Pasternak, who wrote a marvellous novel after a lifetime of writing lyric poetry, has to be shown as belonging 'to our self-conscious age which has, after all, succeeded in diminishing the status of the poet'. *Dr Zhivago* is called 'a burial ground of poetry'; no evidence is given for this extraordinary statement, except a few disjointed remarks that Pasternak made to some woman who pestered him for an interview. ('I believe that it is no longer possible for lyric poetry to express the immensity of our experience. Life has grown too cumbersome, too complicated.') Against that stands the entire weight of the novel itself, with its poet-hero, its frequent meditations on poetry, its use of poetic rather than novelistic methods, and its offering of Zhivago's lyrics as the crown of the whole experience. Mr Peterkiewicz feels all this, and puts his hesitations into the question. 'How sure was he, in fact, about sacrificing poetry for prose?' But he leaves it as a question. The result is to convey the impression, to a hasty reader, that Pasternak's testimony of faith in poetry was in fact an expression of doubt.

So I could cavil on. What makes the book fascinating to me, in spite of its bias, is precisely the wide gulf between Mr Peterkiewicz's pre-assumptions and mine. All of us who are interested in a subject need an occasional reminder that it isn't only *our* approach that brings out the interest and significance of that subject. Mr Peterkiewicz manages to convince me over again of the importance of poetry in the human scheme of things, although—or perhaps because—his approach is overwhelmingly negative. In chapter after chapter, he catalogues the reasons why it is all too easy for a poet to fail, to be overtaken by silence and darkness. Chapter IV, 'Language as Experience', is a good case in point. Many poets feel that there is a wisdom inherent in language itself and that by an intuitive and supple use of the language they can release this wisdom to play its part in the world. Metaphorical language, in particular, is often felt to be not so much invention as the discovery of real correspondences, the uncovering of a system of relatedness that is actually, objectively there in the nature of things. Mr Peterkiewicz rejects this in the name of Time. Since any original metaphor signalizes an intense moment of perception, the almost blinding flash when we perceive a correspondence, it holds good for that moment only. Quoting with approval Wallace Stevens' remark that 'Accuracy of observation is the equivalent of accuracy of thinking', he goes on severely—

This undoubtedly brings the poet's metaphoric vision near to that of the scientist who sees beyond the accepted cliché of colour and shape. If so, metaphor must imply renewed discovery and otherwise can hardly be expected, on its own, to prolong the life of some static moment, any more than language alone can be *aere perennius.*

Therefore:

Once metaphor is understood to be the experience of an intense moment or the instantaneous contact of two images, its survival value will depend on the extent to which it can be catalogued, attached to a period or a stylistic convention.

In other words, all poetic flesh is grass. Once again we come back to the theme that poetry doesn't last, withers away, changes, wobbles, vanishes. Mr Peterkiewicz views bleakly any theory of poetry-as-discovery because what is discovered immediately starts to recede in time, so that the job has to be done again, perpetually.

The effect of this kind of argument is, in the end, tonic. It gives one an increased sense of the difficulty of poetry, the discipline and concentration and sheer *luck* that one needs to write good poems. Even if Mr Peterkiewicz is perpetually treading on the very verge of his own argument, so that one expects to turn the page and find the conclusive argument, stated at last, that will prove poetry to be impossible, that in itself is stimulating; it provokes a spirit of revolt in which one cries out that poetry is alive, that time-bound human beings *can* produce art which is time-bound like themselves and is nevertheless valid.

But the chief service performed by Mr Peterkiewicz's sombre book is without doubt his insistence on poetry as a spiritual discipline. At present, we are going through a flabby, soggy period of instant poetry; the concentration and intensity of art are discarded altogether in favour of a genial incontinence. The poet is seen more and more as a person who appears in public and strikes attitudes. As rhetoric disappears from political life (politicians would lose votes nowadays if they made speeches instead of chatting cosily on television) it seems to be making a back-stairs re-entry via the 'poetry reading'. Certainly the turns that go down best at the average poetry reading are less like poetry than like the kind of speeches politicians used to make at the hustings fifty years ago, plus a larding of obscenities to make them 'modern'.

In social terms, this kind of poetry is worth a diagnostic glance. At the very least, it provides a useful illustration of the axiom that, while a certain thing may be beneficial, a further degree of the same thing may be harmful. (In some areas this is accepted without argument. Nobody thinks that if one aspirin does you good, fifty will do you fifty times as much good.) Here, the beneficial thing that has gone wrong is simplicity. Twenty years ago, what poetry needed most was an injection of straightforwardness. It was rare, at that time, to read a new poem which could have been recited to an audience with any hope that they would pick up its meaning. The key to 'success' in the little-magazine world of that time was to pile on the obscurities. If the editor couldn't make head or tail of your poem, he would probably print it, on the grounds that if it was 'difficult' it was probably a genuine poem. Or, at any rate, near enough to pass for one.

The impulse towards openness of texture, which came in during the 1950s, was necessary and liberating. But like most impulses it was carried beyond the point of usefulness. Now, one longs to meet with a new poem that would have to be taken away into a corner and read slowly and carefully. The band-wagoners, often the very same people who were carefully turning out clotted little poems when that was the vogue, have now carried the cult of accessibility to the point where they encourage only banality. Recently I read somewhere about a squabble between a poet and a reviewer. The reviewer had treated the poet harshly and the poet resented it. 'Ah', said the reviewer with the air of a man proving himself right, 'let him take his poems and see if they would hold an audience of young people in Liverpool.' Literary history is full of meaningless directives applied by self-important little critics: *observe the unities! keep out vulgar language! demonstrate sensibility! demonstrate social consciousness! use poetic cadences! use prose cadences!* But I doubt if there has ever been a more fatuous directive than this one. I have no hostility to young people in Liverpool, or anywhere else, but it remains a fact that many of the poems I value most would not, now or in their own day, have held an audience of young people in Liverpool.

In short, the usual thing has happened. A movement which promised liberation has gone too far; it has not only broken the bars off the windows and unlocked the door, it has taken the roof off the building as well, and made it uninhabitable. This is a pity, because the new impulse towards a popular poetry is itself something to be welcomed. Those of us who grew up in the age of Eliot had long given up hope of seeing any such thing. All Eliot's theories about poetry started from the assumption, which he in turn had inherited from the generation before, that a nation's taste in poetry is dictated by a small, highly cultivated minority, whose attitudes are handed down, in an increasingly blurred form, to ever-widening circles below them. So that what Bloomsbury, or the current equivalent of Bloomsbury, thinks good poetry today, the provinces will have ladled down their throats tomorrow. What we have seen in the last ten years is the complete reversal of this. *Via* the folk-protest singers, *via* the star-building media, *via* the poetry-reading that turns into a demonstration and the demonstration that turns into a poetry-reading, *via* the quasi-political building-up of figures like Yevtushenko, what we have seen is a movement *upwards*, in which the popular taste has imposed itself on the metropolitan literary couturiers. By about 1965, the present-day reincarnations of Bloomsbury were quick-witted enough to perceive that they could best serve their own interests by acceding to popular taste rather than trying to lead it. Hence the sudden outbreak of know-nothing populism, the genuflecting to 'young people in Liverpool', *und so weiter.* The trouble with the popular arts has always been their vulnerability to exploitation.

Meanwhile, there are some things to be grateful for. The mere fact that poetry, of whatever standard, is nowadays a popular art and that the young are sympathetic to it, is refreshing. Arnold Bennett remarked that in England the word 'poetry' would disperse a crowd faster than a firehose; if this is no longer true, there is always the chance that some really good poetry might sneak in, as it were, and make its impact among all the *Ersatz.* Another refreshing development is the present-day interest in the long poem.

Poe's directive about the impossibility of the long poem was accepted without demur by modern poets. Yet it has always been more honoured in the breach than the observance. While paying lip-service to the idea that poetry must be so concentrated as to be unbearable in anything but very small doses, poets have in fact continued to write at length. The immensely long narrative poem of the nineteenth century did indeed pass away, but even those poets who most fully accepted modern poetic theories did not feel it essential to confine themselves within twenty or thirty lines. Eliot's *Four Quartets* are not exactly short poems; Wallace Stevens wrote long poems all the way through his career, from 'The Comedian as the Letter C' (between 1914 and 1922) to 'Notes Towards a Supreme Fiction' (written by 1947). Auden, too, was fond of long poems from the beginning; it is only with advancing years that he has become short-winded. Add to this the fact that a reaction against the tight verbal discipline of so much modern poetry was well in motion at least thirty years ago (*cf.* the deliberate casualness and huge output of Brecht), and we can see that the short, concentrated poem never ousted the long poem as markedly as Poe would have expected.

This gives us a clue to the continuous interest shown by other poets in Ezra Pound's *Cantos*. Pound began work on the *Cantos* in 1915, and was still publishing chunks of them as late as 1965. This means that he has been engaged on them for fifty years, or almost three times as long as it took Shakespeare to write his complete works. That half-century has seen many critical attitudes to the *Cantos* come and go. In 1915 Pound was the propagandist and instigator *par excellence*, the man who had set himself to modernise English and American poetry, single-handed if he had to. Ten years later, his reputation was eclipsed by Eliot's, and remained in that eclipse for twenty years. Now, it has emerged again; Eliot is neglected by the young, while an actual majority of younger poets, especially in America, would acknowledge a debt to the *Cantos*. Some of this can be discounted; outsiderdom is in vogue once more, which means that Pound's public image is attractive and Eliot's is most emphatically not. There are also literary reasons, however.

The mechanized intricacy of the modern world has bred a great desire for simplicity and spontaneity. This much is obvious. What is not quite so obvious is that it has also bred a desire for the inchoate. The things we have to deal with from morning till night, from motor-cars to television sets, from skyscrapers to business corporations, are all so *finished*, so remorselessly contrived and carried out to the last detail, that we begin to long for something that is fragmentary and suggestive, something that we can complete for ourselves. Beyond all question, what has made the *Cantos* so attractive in the last half-century is their stop-and-start, jotting quality. The great lyrical and rhetorical passages are appreciated, too, when they occur; but the central pull of the *Cantos* lies elsewhere. We can see this clearly enough if we turn to those long American poems that most obviously derive from the *Cantos*, notably Williams's *Paterson* and Charles Olson's *Maximus Poems.* Neither Williams nor Olson had Pound's gift for taking wing and soaring; their poems remain dogged assemblages of concrete exhibits, interspersed with sermonizing; but this has not prevented their being taken as seriously, and discussed in the same terms, as the *Cantos.* Obviously people find this kind of notebook-writing very attractive. It ministers to a deep need. In view of the notorious obscurity of long passages of the *Cantos* it may sound odd to say that this need is a need for simplicity; yet, if we dismantle an intricate machine and scatter the parts about on a bench, the result is 'simple' compared with the complex system of interacting parts which is the same machine in working order.[1] The *Cantos* offer us the materials for a history of civilization and a critique of its institutions; Pound tells us, of course, exactly what we are to think about everything he brings before us, but we do not necessarily have to accept his directives; in practice, we tend to treat the poem as a living chaos of ideas and information out of which we can make our own world-system.

One sees this same impulse towards simplicity and spontaneity, towards an art which the reader can participate in and complete, in the rather yearning attitude of younger Western *literati* towards Third World poets. Industrialism has done so much harm to the human spirit that it is not surprising to find a special regard being paid to those poets who come from societies that

[1] *Cf.* Donald Davie on 'The Black Mountain Poets', in *The Survival of Poetry* (p. 219): '. . . they are not interested in making their poems self-sufficient, sailing free like so many rockets from the learning that was accumulated only as it were to assist take-off; on the contrary the poems depend on the learning, they emerge from it only to burrow back into it again, the poems depend upon—and are themselves *part* of—the lifelong addiction of the poet to the business of educating himself, *i.e.* the business of understanding the world that he and we are living in.'

have never been fully industrialized, where people are still close to their physical surroundings and their basic work has not been taken over by the machine. In an interview with Pablo Neruda in 1966, the American poet and editor Robert Bly went straight to the point in his first question :

—A great river of images has flowed into your poetry, as well as into the poetry of Lorca, Aleixandre, Vallejo, and Hernández—an outpouring of poetry from the very roots of poetry. Why has the greatest poetry in the twentieth century appeared in the Spanish language?

Neruda replied modestly, willing to make a generous response while at the same time scaling down the large claim to more manageable proportions. But what I find interesting for our present purposes is Mr Bly's claim and the terms in which he couched it. Notice the imagery from nature rather than art—'a great river of images', 'an outpouring of poetry from the very roots'. Mr Bly thinks of Latin Americans and Spaniards as Wordsworth thought of his dalesmen. They are the uncorrupted, who still have natural and spontaneous feelings and a language able to express them. Within our present world context, Mr Bly and people who think like him are probably right, as Wordsworth was probably right. Neruda's work, like that of Octavio Paz, does have a large, hospitable directness that seems able to absorb the untreated material of everyday existence and show it in the colours of the imagination. In this respect Neruda's *Canto General* is significantly different from Pound's *Cantos.* Pound gives us a series of high spots. He picks out key places, key times, key persons in the history of civilization. Neruda is also writing about a whole civilization, but he seems able to let it simply flow through him. There is far more room in his poems than in Pound's for the animals and plants that travel through time as fellow-passengers with man. Since *Canto General*, Neruda has simplified his style and produced a long series of *Odas Elementales*, odes to simpler things. These poems are offered by Neruda as a tribute to 'ordinary people', the straightforward and simple humanity beloved of Communist theorizing.

One wonders, in fact, what such readers make of them, if they read them at all. A simplification on this massive scale is only possible to a subtle and sophisticated mind, and probably only at the end of its career, after a long exploration of the possibilities of rhetoric and ornament. The bedrock simplicities of a poem like Neruda's 'Ode to Salt', for instance, would be entirely beyond the range of a young, inexperienced poet who decided to write very simply of simple things. In his case, the result would be merely insipid. It is because Neruda is a strong and seasoned poet that he can get down to this effective level of simplicity. The parallel, among poets writing in England, would be that utterly unadorned language which Eliot found for some of the most luminous passages in the *Four Quartets*, or the poems that resulted from Yeats's discovery that

there's more enterprise
In walking naked.

In Günter Grass's new novel, *Local Anaesthetic*, the hero pays a long series of visits to his dentist. The dentist has a television set in his surgery to take the patients' minds off what is happening to them. The man watches the television screen and also engages in political debate with the dentist. Sometimes the television set is switched on, sometimes it is not, but the images that come from the studio and the images that the man's own imagination projects on to the blank screen are equally dream-like and equally compelling. Often, for instance, he sees his ex-fiancée, an attractive girl who left him in a humiliating manner. Sometimes he sees her presenting commercials, and sometimes lying wrapped in cellophane at the bottom of an enormous refrigerator.

The man who is having his teeth cared for is a teacher. One of his students, a generously idealistic lad, is so horrified by the use of napalm by U.S. forces in Viet Nam that he plans, as a protest, to take his pet dachshund on to a fashionable Berlin street, take up a position in full view of a smart café, and there, at the hour of coffee and cream-cakes, souse the animal in petrol and set him alight. The teacher tries to prevent this horrible action. At the same time he is plagued by visions of his own adolescence, when, in the last stages of the war, he roamed the streets as one of a pack of delinquents, committed to the sabotage of the entire grown-up world. Superimposed on all this are the fantasies of his fiancée's father, a retired general just released from years of internment in Russia, who is re-fighting the major battles of the war with scale models in a sandpit, and this time winning them.

I pick out *Local Anaesthetic* for mention because it is worth reading by anyone who still thinks there is a dividing-line between 'the novel' and 'poetry'. It adds up to a very powerful and remarkable picture of one man's mental landscape, and not just any man chosen at random but the characteristic sensitive and intellectual inhabitant of West Germany. All the social realities and the uncomfortable historical legacies are *there*; on the other hand, the continual switching into and out of fantasy, and the pivoting of the story on enormous symbols, take it right out of the domain of that kind of documentary or social-realist novel that would have been, twenty years ago, the natural way of dealing with this kind of subject. Towards the end of the book, there is a passage in which the hero seems to be recollecting the experience of helping his student to set fire to the dog, and being attacked by the crowd, dragged away by the police, thrown into a cell, etc., etc., but there is no indication of any kind whether these things have actually happened or whether he is day-dreaming. This, like the T.V. commercials presented by his ex-fiancée, is simply an example of the kind of thing that, whether it takes place or not, fits naturally into the mental, moral and emotional atmosphere the hero is living in, and which is the real subject of the book.

The dachshund blazing to death in front of the cake-eating ladies, the unattainable girl lying wrapped in cellophane in the deep freeze—these are metaphors, and the ability to communicate primarily in metaphor has generally been thought of as a mark of the poetic mind. Aristotle thought it the special distinguishing mark of the poet that he could create original metaphors, which presumably means that Aristotle would have classed *Local Anaesthetic* as a poem. This kind of writing has put our literary culture into a situation whose full implications have not, I think, been so far taken up by critics. When Frank Kermode, for instance, says that 'in our phase of civility, the novel is the central form of literary art', he seems, for all his polyhistoric scepticism, to be seeing a solid outline of 'the novel' where a practitioner is hard put to it to see anything but a luminous blur.

Or, to put it another way: now that poets seem finally to have abandoned rhyme and metre, pinning their faith in the strength and purity of their images and metaphors ('a great river of images has flowed', etc., etc.), isn't the whole notion of 'poetry', as we have come to know it since the Renaissance, nothing more than a sacrificial lamb waiting for the chopper? If the traditional subject-matter of the novel has been taken over by sociology and reporting, so that the imaginative novelist is forced to make his statements by means of poetic metaphor—that is to say, metaphor no longer hidden under the stucco of 'realism'—how should the poet continue to mark himself off from the imaginative prose-writer? And why should he try to?

Unless, of course, we are moving into an era in which the difference between poetry and fiction will simply be that poetry is oral, that it is disseminated by means of 'poetry-readings' where its main task will be to 'hold an audience of young people in Liverpool'; in which case, after a history of thousands of years, I predict for it a future no longer than the future of the Beatles.

Salute, then, to the makers. And let the ranks be closed.

The Vanishing Critic

IN the literature of the English-speaking world, one thing has been clear for some time: no matter which side of the Atlantic, or which hemisphere, one looks at, the literary critic no longer occupies the centre of the stage. In February 1970, the New York monthly *Commentary* carried an interesting article by Alfred Kazin called 'Whatever happened to Criticism?' Since his argument is a detailed one and concerns itself mainly with the American cultural situation, I will not attempt to go into it here. But he is a fine literary critic who has seen 'the age of criticism' come and go, and now that he has thrown the ball into play, it seems a good moment to give the matter some discussion, from an English as well as an American point of view.

Certainly the age of criticism is over: that age when a handful of critics, mostly employed at universities, formed and cultivated a landscape within which young imaginative talent could grow and could measure its growth. In an interview with the *Paris Review,* Robert Lowell recalled: 'When I was twenty and learning to write, Allen Tate, Eliot, Blackmur, and Winters, and all those people, were very much news. You waited for their essays, and when a good critical essay came out it had the excitement of a new imaginative work.' Lowell was twenty in 1937: my impression is that in England the age of criticism waited another ten years to get going—except, of course, in Cambridge, where the great vogue of I. A. Richards among the young was already at its height in the Twenties.

Mention of Richards, and Cambridge, gives us our initial bearing. The enthusiasm which fuelled the age of criticism came from the young. 'When one says that a writer is fashionable,' George Orwell noted, 'one nearly always means that he is read by people under 30.' Between 1945 and 1960 a body of literary criticism, written mostly by middle-aged men, had a profound effect on 'people under 30'. Now, no such phenomenon exists. What was it about the young then that made them so interested in criticism? And what is it about the young today that makes them no longer interested?[1]

Since we must start somewhere, let us begin with the fact that the young in the Fifties were much less politicized than they are now. The energies which now go into 'direct action' and the striking of revolutionary attitudes went, then, into other things. Not that we in those days were 'apathetic', as is so often said. Our concern for the problems of the society was just as keen as anyone's today. The difference was that our concern did not feel the urgent need to issue in direct action. We tended to assume that the actual engineering of social change, by means of legislation and so forth, could best be left to professionals; we believed that what a civilization needs is the right quality of *feeling*. To respond to life with one's emotional priorities in the right order—that was the ideal. A society that could no longer react to cruelty and injustice, because these things had become so commonplace as to be accepted; or a society so clogged with greed that its ever-expanding material appetites pushed everything else to one side; or a society so drowned in unreality, in the *suggestio falsi* of advertising or the *suppressio veri* of sedative entertainment, that it lulled its citizens into a trance—all these were to be resisted, and they could be resisted without smashing a single embassy window or cracking the ribs of a single policeman, simply by taking every opportunity to promote a wholeness of vision, and an honesty of response, that would enable

[1] John Updike, in a story 'One of My Generation' (*Dialogue*, iv, 4, 1971) amusingly hits off the feelings of a middle-aged writer, once an 'English major', facing an audience of present-day students: 'Could I explain, to a crowd of riot-minded guitarists . . . with what zest we executed the academic exercise, by now perhaps as obsolete as diagrammatic parsing, called *explication*? To train one's mind to climb, like a vine on a sunny wall, across the surface of a poem by George Herbert, seeking the handhold crannies of pun, ambiguity, and buried allusion; to bring forth from the surface sense of the poem an altogether other hidden poem of consistent metaphor and, as it were, verbal subversion; to feel, in Eliot's phrase, a thought like an emotion; to *explicate*—this was life lived on the nerve ends.'

life to be lived meaningfully. And when asked where this wholeness, this honesty, were demonstrated, our answer was: 'In major literature—in the great books, past and present, which make up our tradition.'

This was a view that put a great strain on literature, but then that strain had always been put on it, and since the days of Matthew Arnold the pressure had steadily increased, and literature was bearing up well. Arnold's notion, that religion has been dethroned and that the official repository of human values will henceforth be in imaginative literature, has been attacked from various angles, but that has not stopped it from becoming widely accepted; it could fairly be said to be the view of most people in the modern world. (By 'most people', as usual, I mean 'most of the small proportion, probably one in every hundred thousand of the human race, who think about these problems at all'.) What followed naturally was that a great strain was also put on the critic. Imaginative literature works largely by metaphor, and the interpretation of metaphor cannot be a cut-and-dried affair. (After 2000 years of ceaseless exposition, there is still no universally accepted interpretation of the parables of Jesus, for instance. Nor can there be.) If spiritual health resided in literature, this made literary study into a kind of religion, and a religion must have its priesthood. The quarrels of priests, the *odium theologicum*, are notorious; the quarrels of literary critics became hardly less so.

Arnold himself was a formidable controversialist; T. S. Eliot, in his criticism the chief intermediary between Arnold and the moderns, also knew very well how to undermine an opponent's position; and this tradition, already strongly imbued with the spirit of controversy and even of satire, came to us via the strong and idiosyncratic personalities of a number of brilliant teacher-critics—notably Richards, Leavis, Empson. All these, in one way or another, were attackers. Richards's work, from the early Twenties onwards, was understood to apply a steadily destructive pressure to the assumptions of the old liberal-humanist education which was eclectic, founded on good taste and class solidarity, and not given to strenuous thinking. Empson, beginning as Richards's most brilliant pupil, also brought new ideas and new rigours to bear on the old cake-crust of 'taste', and in his case there was also the long-sustained quarrel with Christianity, giving his work a specially acerbic flavour in an epoch when criticism from a Christian standpoint was enjoying much favour. But it was, of course, F. R. Leavis who most sharply typified in our minds the ideal of the independent critic as controversialist, carrying on year by year a stubborn resistance to a vaguely-outlined but powerful 'Establishment' whose influence was constantly felt both in the academic and the metropolitan literary worlds. So that the smartness of London weekly journalism and the epigrams of an Oxbridge dinner-party came to be felt, by a whole generation, as manifestations of one and the same sinister power working for the suppression of everything genuine in life and literature.

I have long felt, looking back, that there was an unnecessarily melodramatic flavour to all this. As I suggested years ago in a retrospect of this period (in *Sprightly Running*), academic people tend to form into small clusters and isolate themselves from the larger scene; they then view that scene with suspicion through a rather small view-finder, and see conspiracy where the rest of us see only muddle and incompetence. Dr Leavis, during those years, used sometimes to talk as if the modish fatuities of smart journalism were uttered in the interests of a conspiracy directed primarily at himself, whereas the people who uttered them probably thought, for all that week and part of the next, that they were enunciating important truths. Nor do I, any longer, believe in a monolithic literary and cultural 'Establishment', cunningly intent on fostering its own values. What I have seen of people in important positions in the literary and academic worlds has never convinced me that they are sufficiently intelligent, or sufficiently capable of sinking their individual differences and rivalries, to co-operate to that extent. So the quarrels and alliances and denunciations of those days, when one re-reads them now, have a yellowed air. But they were very important at the time. Young people enjoy drama; they need to feel that they are proving themselves by bravely attacking something powerful; they also need to feel that by sweeping away the corruption of the last generation, they are preparing a better world. These are right instincts, and if the literary criticism of those days helped to foster and canalize them, then so much the better for it. To us, then, it seemed that literary criticism was a truly central activity, relevant to every area of human life. It was serious, it was constructive, and because of its gladiatorial element it was also exciting.

Up to now, I have been writing from experience and with a fair certainty of what I am talking about. The rest of this article, which will try to assign reasons for the disappearance of these attitudes, ought really to be written by a member of the new generation. But since this is in practice rather difficult to arrange, I will continue, but it must be understood that we are now modulating into guesswork.

One change is obvious. Our attitude in 1945-60 was based on the assumption that the book was at the centre of our culture; and in the culture of the Seventies the book is no longer at the centre. It is still conspicuously present—people who predict that the book will simply disappear never explain how we are going to manage without it, even in the practical business of life—but it is no longer at the centre. All the arts of language are to some extent in eclipse, because this is an age that communicates primarily by images. At our universities, we now have a generation of students brought up entirely within the television era. They were the toddlers who saw ten thousand hours of television before they read their first word. Is it surprising that the art that seems natural to them is not literature but the cinema? Or that young poets now write a kind of loose-knit verse which presents carefully chosen images in carelessly chosen words?

Add to that the information explosion. The effect of being bombarded with news and documentary, the continuous walloping with what-is-happening-now, is to make it impossible to keep one's bottom in a chair. Such a barrage of stimuli calls for action, action and more action. I read recently an article by some trend-monger (in, I think, the *Evergreen Review*) about the literary taste of the young: one of his findings was that the young simply didn't read novels at all. In view of the frantic pace of events as presented to them by the media, imaginative fiction cannot react fast enough. The months of patient craftsmanship that have to go into a novel inevitably mean that, as a reaction to a specific situation, it is neither spontaneous enough nor immediate enough. What is wanted is the poem that can be written in an hour, recited in ten minutes at a poetry-reading, and replaced by another poem in time for next week's reading. Literature of the throw-away age, instantly replaceable, not intended to survive in the mind because the mind that harbours such jetsam must be living in the past—this is where the television age has brought us.

When I am pressed to give a definition of criticism, I find the safest and most reliable is one coined by Frank Kermode: 'the medium in which past work survives'. This would include every possible means of assessing a work of art, from cocktail-party chatter to scholarly investigation. And if not a final definition of criticism, this is certainly an essential preliminary definition. Somewhere within it is all the worst and silliest criticism, but also all the best and wisest. But what happens in a society which does not *want* past work to survive? Nothing could be simpler than to find and re-read a book published twenty years ago. But how do you set about seeing a film made twenty years ago? It might come your way by luck, especially if it is a film that has been talked and written about enough ('the medium in which past work survives' . . .), but it can be taken as absolutely certain that most of the films of twenty years ago will never be available again; or the television programmes; or the radio programmes. And if the past is not available, there is nothing against which we can measure the present, and one of the main traditional activities of the critic has gone.

Faced with this situation, criticism has two alternatives. One is to go about its business, in the hope of retaining the attention of a public large enough to play some part in shaping our society. To recognize, in short, that though the critic may never again be a star and a *prima donna*, he may have valuable work to do in the world. The other alternative is to desert the criticism of books in favour of the criticism of social tendencies: to produce that smart, rather vaporous politico-cultural journalism which scorns to anchor itself to anything as solid and unchanging as a book, where the reader can check his own impressions against the critic's, and concentrates instead on 'the scene'. Not that writing about 'the scene' is in itself a disgraceful activity. Not that it is not worth doing. But the rush to analyse 'trends', the scramble to get away from printed texts, which stand still, and run after the whizzing comets of where-it's-at, is disturbing because it shows a willingness to abandon the search for standards. The person who recalls our attention to some important book is helping to steady our minds: the person who foretells the intellectual fashion of the week after next is helping to unsettle them.

This unsettlement will probably be seen as something positive by those to whom the past is merely a dead weight, and tradition an obstructive humbug. The idea of tradition was a battleground in modern criticism for fifty years; when the early modern poets began writing, they were opposed by a generation of late-Victorians to whom tradition meant doing things in the way that had been good enough for your father and your grandfather—the 'continuous literary decorum' that Bridges found wanting in Hopkins. Since this notion of tradition was obviously hampering, the more thoughtful of the modernists took pains to think out a more constructive view of tradition, best perceived and most lucidly stated by T. S. Eliot. In fact Eliot's criticism, from 'Tradition and the Individual Talent' onwards, radiates chiefly from his sense of a relationship with the past; and it was essentially Eliot's idea of tradition that was documented and enforced by Leavis and the *Scrutiny* group. It seemed natural, in those days, to see the present as nourished by the past.

Now, suddenly, to large numbers of people, it no longer does seem natural. It is quite common to meet people in their twenties, often well-read and highly intelligent, who genuinely feel that the present age is so different from anything that went before that the bridges have been dynamited and nothing can come over to us from the past. To these people, their own continent

Radio Till Now

We are supposed to be living in an epoch in which television has supplanted radio. Yet as long as radio exists at all, the take-over can never be quite complete. It is impossible to feel the same respect for the younger medium.

Radio, after all, has glorious things in its history. Not only has it pioneered many important developments in education—both in the narrower and the wider sense of that term—but it has an heroic dimension. Brave men, hiding in barns and attics, have defied tyranny by means of radio. Its equipment is cheap, portable, and easy to hide; that of television is complex, heavy, and costly. The Gestapo in occupied Europe were effectively hindered and baited by means of radio, and if the miniature transistor set had been invented in those days the resistance might well have been even more formidable. Television will never come to the aid of freedom in this way. A pirate television set is an impossibility; its whereabouts would be spotted before the equipment was half set up. Again, radio can work *for* the law as well as, if necessary, against it. As an infant medium, only a few months off the drawing-board, it showed that it meant business by securing the arrest of Crippen on board an Atlantic liner.

By comparison, television has nothing to show except the closed-circuit scanning of department stores. It belongs, irredeemably, to the world of merchandise. That is why commercial television seemed a natural, if depressing, development; whereas a commercial radio network, such as we are about to have slung round our necks by Mr Christopher Chataway and his accomplices, seems the debasement of something noble, like those circus acts in which lions jump through paper hoops.

If radio is murdered, it will be an inside job. The medium will be overshadowed by television, but never eclipsed altogether, so long as radio 'to itself do rest but true'. In England, what this boils down to is that the sound-broadcasting side of the BBC must be no further humiliated and pestered by the forces of trivialisation and commercialisation, either within the Corporation or on the floor of the House of Commons. For as long as any of us can remember, the BBC has given us the best sound-radio service in the world, and though the dismantling has already gone very far, we must, as a nation, firmly insist that it shall go no further.

One of the most active contributors to radio, during the golden years of its ascendancy, was D. G. Bridson.[1] In thirty-five working years he produced, or wrote, or originated in one way or another, over eight hundred broadcasts, many of which were acknowledged classics of radio. An early effort of his, *The March of the '45*, a sound-panorama of the Jacobite Rising, became one of the BBC's favourite show-case exhibits; for years it was studied by all producers attending the BBC Staff Training School—which meant, since these people came from many countries and often returned home after training, that its influence was world-wide. Mr Bridson's particular combination of gifts was well suited to make him a pioneer in this kind of programme: an accomplished writer of verse of the immediate, speakable kind, he had a strong historical imagination and a grasp of large effects which could be blocked out in sound. In the case of *The March of the '45*, he seems to have been fortunate in his Scottish collaborators:

. . . undoubtedly the impact of the programme on listeners was mainly due to the inspired production of the Scottish cast by Gordon Gildard. Only when the story moved south of the border did Harding and I take up the thread with the march from Carlisle down to Derby. The final third of the show, from Falkirk to Culloden, was Gildard's responsibility again. I have had many exciting moments in radio but few so strangely exciting as my first hearing of what he had done with the verse. As declaimed by the Scottish narrators, Douglas Allen and Rex de la Haye, it came down the line from Glasgow like a highland river in spate. This was radio

[1] *Prospero and Ariel: the Rise and Fall of Radio. A personal Recollection.* By D. G. Bridson.

with all the stops out—crowds, fights, orchestra, choir and gunfire, adding their quota to the effect.

'Radio with all the stops out', crowds, pipes, orchestra, gunfire—this, one feels, is where Mr Bridson's heart lay and still lies. (The same zest comes into his narrative where he describes the experience of recording the Zulu Royal Dance at Eshowe.) He is a natural Features man, at home in the territory where imaginative writing mingles with journalism and documentary.

I do not mean to enforce a hampering distinction here: it is not my opinion that art, any more than science, ought to observe a rigid boundary between Pure and Applied; nevertheless, it is a fact that in art, as in science, there will be no first-rate Applied unless there is some first-rate Pure to nourish it and keep it up to standard. One's cavil against Bridson is that he is too much an Applied man; strong in those skills that strikingly project a point of view or sketch a social scene, much weaker in everything that concerns the purer reaches of art. The literary asides in this book show a commonplace taste and an acceptance of superficial reputations which would, I think, have prevented Bridson from doing really memorable work as a pure writer, within radio or without it. His real gift was for the bold, provocative statement that opened people's ears and eyes. In the 1930s, when the North of England was a vast shadow-area into which few members of the governing class had ever ventured, and which endured a great deal of quite unnecessary suffering merely because it was invisible from the Home Counties, Bridson did excellent work with such programmes as his 'Harry Hopeful' series. His object then was to 'project the North', an aim he was well qualified to achieve. One becomes more dubious when, thirty years later, one finds him still 'projecting', still interested in causing a stir and waking people up. In his marathon series of twenty programmes, *America Since the Bomb*, Bridson prided himself on presenting a lively impression of American social unrest and political dissent, an impression that was not lost on the British young. He tells us, with a touch of complacency, that one of its constituent programmes, *Revolt on the Campus*, included 'a truly inspiring outburst by Norman Mailer', as if Mailer's predictable outbursts could still, at that time of day, inspire anybody. He gives us a roll-call of 'the names that the series threw up as its heroes', including Kerouac, Ginsberg, Ferlinghetti, and others of the same well-shuffled pack of cards whose influence has gone so far to produce the flood of mediocrity in which the literary scene is currently awash. To be blunt, Bridson's acceptance of all this over-excited *kitsch* was much too uncritical, and when he congratulates himself on being so closely in touch with Youth, one begins almost to associate him with all the other middle-aged misleaders who have served young people so shabbily in the last ten years.

With its portrayal of student unrest, social non-conformism, anti-war demonstrations and political militancy, *America since the Bomb* gave a strong foretaste of British unrest in the years that followed it, the later 'sixties. And I was glad to feel that even as I approached the 'sixties myself, I could still mount radio exciting to the younger audience. The correspondence that I have from the series, and the steady requests for scripts from the universities, persuaded me that I had done so.

Perhaps one day it will become clear that the people who served the student generation most honestly, during the troubled period which began about 1965 and still continues, were those who prevailed on it to slow down long enough to think for a moment, rather than rush out into the streets and start screaming and throwing things, however 'exciting to the younger audience' such eruptions might be.

I say these distasteful things not to knock down Bridson—if he is not equally perceptive over the whole range of his activities, not equally on his guard against all forms of self-deception, which of us is?—but to indicate that the limitations of his vision have their effect on the picture he gives us of radio, of its history up till now, and of its future. He sub-titles his book 'A Personal Recollection', but even with this candid disclaimer it is hard for the reader to keep constantly in view the fact that he is writing most of the time not about radio in general but about the radio Feature. If one sits back and thinks about everything that British radio achieved, the great wealth and diversity it brought to us, between 1930 and 1950, and then turns back to Bridson's pages, it becomes apparent that not only much, but *most*, of that wealth finds no mention there. The whole gigantic effort, an effort largely successful, to spread a taste for good music, when Sir Walford Davies, Master of the King's Music, showed himself to be the first and finest of a long line of gifted popularisers; the radiance of those variety shows, all the way from 'Band-Wagon', through 'Itma' to the Goons; the political drama that was acted out over the loudspeakers throughout the 1930s and forties, when radio was the world's most important medium for oratory (if the radio-borne yells of Hitler gave the thirties their dimension of nightmare, the bulldog-growl of Churchill likewise flavoured the war years). Mr Bridson's book has a lengthy index, but an index at least equally long could be made up of names that became nationally famous through radio, from Tommy Handley to Spike Hughes, from C. E. M. Joad to C. S. Lewis, for which one looks in vain.

Mr Bridson's theme is 'the rise *and fall* of radio', and the point I am trying to make is that if he had not been so whole-heartedly a Features man, the fall might not have seemed so complete. To him, when Features Department was axed and its large and shining galaxy of writers and producers dispersed, it must have seemed like the end of the road for radio. Yet surely if radio is to resist being gobbled up by television, it must work for survival in those areas where it is strongest and most valuable. And the feature programme is the wrong ground to fight over, if only because it is exactly the kind of programme which television can do as well or better.

I speak of radio's being 'gobbled up' by television, and my definition of such gobbling would be the taking-over by TV of *all* radio's functions, whether or not it can do them better. When people switch on TV to get the news, or to hear music, or any and every time they want to hear a story told or a song sung, then TV has won, but it is a hollow victory because it involves being burdened with so much material that is not suitable for the screen at all, with the accompanying frustration and waste of resources.

At the moment, radio in England is far better than TV in its news coverage; programmes like 'The World at One', 'Ten o' Clock', 'News Desk' are better than their equivalents on the screen, while the invaluable 'From Our Own Correspondent' on Saturday mornings has the depth and thoughtfulness that used to be characteristic of a paper like *The Times* in its great days. The 'music programme', with its non-stop presentation of a very wide range of good music, supplies another need; Mr Bridson despises it because it means hiving off the listeners who want real music on to a separate wavelength, leaving the populace to be permanently peppered with pullulating pop. 'It has merely made doubly sure', he writes, 'that none but the already converted will ever hear good music again'. But surely this attitude is a hang-over from the days when the BBC saw itself as the great coaxer, the nanny with the medicine on a lump of sugar, slipping the Beethoven in between the banalities. I am certain that this was the right policy thirty years ago, when the whole machinery in culture-diffusion was in the Spinning Jenny stage, and there were millions of people who would never have known what a symphony orchestra sounded like if they had not had it trickled into their ears unawares. But presumably that strategy, if successful, was bound to become obsolete; it was designed to work towards a state of affairs beyond itself, and I think it has done so.

Mr Bridson also dislikes 'Radio 3'—the music station—because he associates it with the assassination of the Third Programme. But my impression is that, here, a stealthy but successful rearguard action has been fought. After about eight o'clock at night, the rule compelling Radio 3 to put out nothing but music, or talk about music, is evidently in abeyance, and a good deal of Third Programme material is broadcast every evening.

Radio drama is also a strongly continuing form, and in Mr Bridson's silence on that topic—a neglect so striking that it seems almost wilful—I wonder if we are not in the presence of some last remnant of an ancient rivalry between Features and Drama. The whole question of the radio play is, in any case, one that could do with a good airing. (The play on words is unintentional, but let it stand.)

Radio drama is an excellent form. It sets an interesting challenge to the writer, the producer, and the actor; while to the listener, it allows the blessing of being able to use his own imagination instead of having everything relentlessly imagined *for* him. There is a general principle here. Those arts which leave the recipient's imagination something to complete, instead of making him a passive consumer, are better than those which present him with a totally finished and packaged product. E.g., the novel is better than the film; within the sphere of film, the silent cinema was better than the talkies; the radio play is better than the TV play; stylized marionettes are better than waxworks.

To the writer, and to anyone interested in the arts of language, the radio play has a particular importance because it is a verbal medium. The modern writer so often finds himself seduced away from his desk, taking part in activities which are essentially corporate, in which those things he has uniquely to offer are not likely to be of much use. Both film and television use writers, but they use them as ideas men. The most justly celebrated writer, when he enters a film studio, finds himself rated fairly low down in the organisation : a little above the studio carpenter, perhaps, but a long way below the chief cameraman and the lighting specialist. This may be good for him if what he needs is to be taken down a peg, but I cannot help feeling that in the world as it is today what most writers need is to be moved up a few pegs. There cannot have been any age in which the arts of language, the pure gift of narration and evocation *in words*, have been so little regarded. Hundreds of thousands of students are taken on guided tours through 'lit.' by a large corps of well-paid instructors, but the said instructors do not seem to have much success in revealing to the young the depth and power, the mystery and beauty, of language, and the arts of language. As soon as they are released from their studies, they turn back like sun-flowers towards the glare of the lighted and animated image.

In this situation, the radio play can make a great contribution. It can keep alive the concept of language as an independent medium—liberated from print, yes, but not having to pay the price that film and TV exact for that liberation. The BBC, or some individuals within the BBC, appear to me to have grasped this very well. In recent years, radio has presented important new work by such writers as Beckett and Pinter; and run-of-the-mill radio drama, the soil in which the masterpieces can take root, continues to go out week by week.

As I write, a film production of *Under Milk Wood* is in full swing. Because the very perfection of *Under Milk Wood* as a radio play makes it unsuitable for any other medium, the adaptor has gone over it with a mental crowbar, finding places where he can force it open and inject material taken from elsewhere in Dylan Thomas's writings. This urge to smash perfection and reassemble the pieces in some grotesquely crippled form seems to be a purely twentieth-century phenomenon. Instead of making a film *ab ovo*, reflecting the same vision of life as *Under Milk Wood*, if that is what's wanted, this team has to take a perfect radio play and butcher it. I hope the BBC will mount a production of the play in its true and original form, and put it out in the same week that the film has its *première*.[1] Actors of the stature of Hugh Griffith are available, and there are still some producers who know how to get the best out of a brilliant cast round the microphone. I do not believe that sound drama is dead—but even if it were, I don't see why we should have to endure the spectacle of its corpse being dragged at the heels of the film industry.

[1] They didn't.

PART TWO

The Writers

Orwell in the Thirties

> The great works by which, not only in literature, art, and science generally, but in religion itself, the human spirit has manifested its approaches to totality, and to a full, harmonious perfection, and by which it stimulates and helps forward the world's general perfection, come, not from Nonconformists, but from men who either belong to Establishments or have been trained in them.
>
> MATTHEW ARNOLD

> If there is one type of man to whom I feel myself inferior, it is a coal miner
>
> GEORGE ORWELL

I

MOST of what seem to be the paradoxes in Orwell's thinking and writing can be explained by the fact that he was born into an age in which the really suffocating nonsense was talked by reactionaries, and lived on into an age in which it was talked by progressives.

Orwell was born into the Edwardian age and seems to have started his life with an unusually thorough and unpleasant immersion in the character-forming processes of that age at their silliest. The relevant documents here are the autobiographical sections of *The Road to Wigan Pier* (i.e., chapters 8 and 9) and the essay 'Such, Such Were the Joys' (1947), describing his prep school. The portraits of 'Sambo' and 'Flip', the headmaster of 'St Cyprian's' and his wife, are good enough to stand as a classic case-history of English snobbery of the kind that flourished in the afterglow of Victorian confidence and died out only sporadically, being still alive in pockets well into the nineteen-fifties and probably not entirely extinct, in a duck-billed platypus sort of way, even now. Their ministrations enabled Orwell to go to Eton by means of a scholarship, which presumably did him some good or at least no harm (while very scathing about his upbringing in general, he seems to have had no bitter memories of Eton itself), but on the other hand they placed on his back a psychological load which he had to spend years trying to shake off. He was a late developer, a fact which can fairly certainly be traced to those appalling years at St Cyprian's in which he was flogged, like a half-grown racehorse, to run faster and faster while resentment smouldered within him and became fiercer with every year. At least, he promised himself, he would slacken off once he had got past 'the exam'—a resolve which, as he tells us, 'was so fully carried out that between the ages of thirteen and twenty-two or three I hardly ever did a stroke of avoidable work'.

Beyond this personal grievance there lay a wider rejection of the whole glittering world of social and material success which Flip and Sambo were supposed to be putting within the grasp of their fortunate *protégés.* Looking back, he saw them as 'a couple of silly, shallow, ineffectual people, eagerly clambering up a social ladder which any thinking person could see to be on the point of collapse'. But even if that ladder had been eternal, the happy land to which it led was repulsive to Orwell. In view of the current tendency to see the Edwardian age as a golden afternoon, it is worth recalling how it appeared to Orwell, who had, as a clever schoolboy of the scholarship-winning type, experienced that age almost as it might have been experienced by a member of the working class—that is, as a series of burdens laid on his back in the name of nothing very much.

There never was, I suppose, in the history of the world a time when the sheer vulgar fatness of wealth, without any kind of aristocratic elegance to redeem it, was so obtrusive as in those years before 1914. It was the age when crazy millionaires in curly top-hats and lavender waistcoats gave champagne parties in rococo house-boats on the Thames, the age of diabolo and hobble skirts, the age of the 'knut' in his grey bowler and cutaway coat, the age of *The Merry Widow*, Saki's novels, *Peter Pan* and *Where the Rainbow Ends*, the age when people talked about chocs and cigs and ripping and topping and heavenly, when they went for divvy week-ends at Brighton and had scrumptious teas at the Troc. From the whole decade before 1914 there seems to breathe forth a smell of the more vulgar, un-grown-up kinds of luxury, a smell of brilliantine and *crème-de-menthe* and soft-centred chocolates—an atmosphere, as it were, of eating everlasting strawberry ices on green lawns to the tune of the Eton Boating Song. The extraordinary thing was the way in which everyone took it for granted that this oozing, bulging wealth of the English upper and upper-middle classes would last for ever, and was part of the order of things.

The same note was struck in the essay on Wells (1941):

When Wells was young, the antithesis between science and reaction was not false. Society was ruled by narrow-minded, profoundly incurious people, predatory businessmen, dull squires, bishops, politicians who could quote Horace but had never heard of algebra. Science was faintly disreputable and religious belief obligatory. Traditionalism, stupidity, snobbishness, patriotism, superstition and love of war seemed to be all on the same side; there was need of someone who could state the opposite point of view. Back in the nineteen-hundreds it was a wonderful experience for a boy to discover H. G. Wells. There you were, in a world of pedants, clergymen and golfers, with your future employers exhorting you to 'get on or get out', your parents systematically warping your sexual life, and your dull-witted schoolmasters sniggering over their Latin tags; and here was this wonderful man who could tell you about the inhabitants of the planets and the bottom of the sea, and who *knew* that the future was not going to be what respectable people imagined.

As if the kind of upbringing we glimpse here were not enough, the young Orwell went straight from Eton into the Imperial Police in Burma, where he had to do the dirty work of Empire with his own hands. Five years of this were enough: on his first home leave, he resigned. Once again, he sums up for us with great penetration the nature of what had been done to him.

I was conscious of an immense weight of guilt that I had got to expiate. I suppose that sounds exaggerated; but if you do for five years a job that you thoroughly disapprove of, you will probably feel the same. I had reduced everything to the simple theory that the oppressed are always right and the oppressors are always wrong: a mistaken theory, but the natural result of being one of the oppressors yourself. I felt that I had got to escape not merely from imperialism but from every form of man's dominion over man. I wanted to submerge myself, to get right down among the oppressed, to be one of them and on their side against their tyrants. And, chiefly because I had had to think everything out in solitude, I had carried my hatred of oppression to extraordinary lengths. At that time failure seemed to me to be the only virtue. Every suspicion of self-advancement, even to 'succeed' in life to the extent of making a few hundreds a year, seemed to me spiritually ugly, a species of bullying.

As a picture of Orwell in 1927, this is entirely credible. Behind him were the austerities of his 'lower-upper-middle-class' home, Flip and Sambo, Eton ('five years in a lukewarm bath of snobbery' is his casual summing-up of all Public School education, and he does not exempt his *alma mater* though he does not go out of his way to savage her, either), and then Burma, the monsoons, the convicts, the hangings, the mindlessly rigid society at the Club, and the endless involvement in futile situations such as that captured so perfectly in 'Shooting an Elephant'.

It was these experiences that gave Orwell the head of steam that drove him into the thirties. Books like *Down and Out in Paris and London*, *Burmese Days*, *A Clergyman's Daughter*, are straight expressions of the resentment, the guilt, the stinging pity for those pinned to the earth by 'the system', that one would expect to see engendered by these means in a young man whose mind was both strong and sensitive. And during these years it was very natural that Orwell should identify the enemy as being on the Right. Socialism was the answer, if an answer in political terms were to be found at all. And Orwell was determined that it could and must. Throughout his life he never wavered from his attitude of stern contempt for those who claimed that the nobler destiny was to be above the battle. A decent society would never come unless men got down and worked for it—even, if necessary, fought for it.

This was the Orwell who saw himself unequivocally as a man of the Left, and who felt it his duty as a writer to champion the underdog in the rich and technically advanced societies of the West. Naturally, he had misgivings, but these were of a personal, temperamental nature. To identify yourself with any cause is, inevitably, to be dismayed at some of the people you find yourself trying to co-operate with. Hence the amusing knockabout at the end of *The Road to Wigan Pier.* Orwell had been conscientiously trying to fit himself into the framework of Socialism, and he had found a good deal of smugness, evasiveness, selective blindness, and sheer muddle there—as one finds in any mass movement. In addition, there was the usual disagreement about objectives. Orwell was for a simple version of Socialism which boiled down to (*a*) fairer distribution of wealth and resources and (*b*) large-scale concerted resistance to international Fascism. And he rightly realized that many people describing themselves as Socialists, and holding influential positions within the world of Socialism, were lukewarm about these objectives and seemed to have other, unconfessed objectives of their own :

> Sometimes I look at a Socialist—the intellectual, tract-writing type of Socialist, with his pullover, his fuzzy hair, and his Marxian quotation—and wonder what the devil his motive really *is.* It is often difficult to believe that it is a love of anybody, especially of the working class, from whom he is of all people the furthest removed. The underlying motive of many Socialists, I believe, is simply a hypertrophied sense of order. The present state of affairs offends them not because it causes misery, still less because it makes freedom impossible, but because it is untidy; what they desire, basically, is to reduce the world to something resembling a chess-board.

Orwell's misgivings about the Left, however vigorously he expressed them, had by the beginning of 1937 not yet attained the status of a 'disillusion'. We can, indeed, already see the tiny hair-line cracks which were soon to open out into major rifts.

But, for the moment, it is a matter of disagreement about emphases rather than opposing structures of values. The Introduction which Victor Gollancz was fain to provide before *Wigan Pier* could be trusted into the hands of Left Book Club members is still part of that world of innocent knockabout. Orwell's suspicion of Stalin's methods, for instance, provokes Gollancz to a plaintive look-here-I-say that reminds one of Boswell's protest that Johnson was surely going too far in condemning the slave trade. Noting Orwell's 'general dislike of Russia', Gollancz goes on wonderingly: 'he even commits the curious indiscretion of referring to Russian commissars as "half-gramophones, half-gangsters".' Such was the state of mind of the British intelligentsia at that time. Russia was a country calling itself 'Socialist' and Russia was industrializing rapidly, so Russia *had* to be right. To see the commissars for what they were was at worst a counter-revolutionary crime and at best a 'curious indiscretion' like swearing in front of some white-haired old vicar.

The time was now approaching, however, when Orwell's condemnation of totalitarian methods within the Left was to go beyond the realm of the 'curious indiscretion'. Up to 1937, Orwell saw the world struggle as between Left and Right, with the goodwill and the good arguments on the side of the Left, if only they could get rid of the tiresome hangers-on who came 'flocking towards the smell of progress like bluebottles to a dead cat'. After 1937, he saw it in terms of democracy *versus* totalitarianism, and he no longer cared whether the totalitarianism called itself Left or Right.[1] What changed his outlook was his Spanish experience. *Homage to Catalonia* is the most important book for anyone who wants to understand Orwell's mind. It is a book that describes the hinge of a man's life.

II

Every tyranny is resisted by two quite distinct groups of people.

[1] Cf. the essay on Arthur Koestler (1944): 'The sin of nearly all left-wingers from 1933 onwards is that they have wanted to be anti-Fascist without being anti-totalitarian.'

There are those who resist the tyranny in the name of freedom, and there are those who resist it in the hope of replacing it by a rival tyranny in which they themselves will enjoy power.

During the years of revolutionary struggle, these two groups can paper over their differences. They can work together, fight together, live as brothers in blood and toil. The moment of truth comes when the original tyranny is overthrown. Immediately the first group, those whose aim is freedom for themselves and others, want to take off the pressure, to begin to relax and be happy, to let the people move at last without their fetters. The answer of the other group, the new tyrants, is invariably the same. Counter-revolutionary forces are at hand, treachery is everywhere, discipline and privation must be harder still, criticism is treason. Within a few months, the lovers of freedom are driven into exile (if they are lucky), exterminated (if they are unlucky), but in either case removed.

Orwell's experiences in the Spanish civil war gave him an inside view of this process actually at work. When that war broke out in 1936, Left-wingers throughout the world felt a sense of exalted dedication. At last the gloves were off. International Fascism, backed by big business, the Church, and reactionary forces of every kind, had launched an armed attack on a pacific and Socialist government. This was the beginning, the first in that series of battles which would sweep Fascism from the earth and leave peace, brotherhood and Socialism. It was a noble ideal, and many believed in it nobly. They gave to it what they had to give—their strength, their courage, their lives.

Of those who died, the lucky ones were those who died in battle. Many others died in crowded Spanish prisons, held *incommunicado* amid dirt and neglect, never understanding from first to last why this was being done to them. In fact, they were casualties not in the war against Fascism, but in the struggle for power within the structure of the Left. The Communists, directed from Moscow, had never any intention of losing that struggle. The men who found themselves in jail, who were denounced as traitors and spies by propagandists in the rear at the very moment when they were facing Fascist bayonets in the front lines, were anarchists, Trotskyites real or so-called, and in general, men of the Left who did not toe the line of the Central Committee.[1]

Twice over, Orwell came within a millimetre of leaving his bones on Spanish soil. First he had a Fascist bullet clean through his neck. Then, when he got out of hospital and was looking forward to a short spell of rest and convalescence in Barcelona before going back into the fighting, he had to hide from the police, skulk in deserted buildings, sleep in the street, and finally bolt across the French border one jump ahead of the agents of the government—that same government for which he had risked and endured so much.

Orwell left a Spain on which the night of a police-state had fallen. 'The arrests, raids, searchings were continuing without pause; practically everyone we knew, except those who were still at the front, was in jail by this time. The police were even boarding the French ships that periodically took off refugees and seizing suspected "Trotskyists".' He got back to an England where nobody wanted to hear his story. To the Right, still busily retailing stories about how government forces employed their leisure time in raping nuns, he was discredited because he had fought on the Socialist side. To the Left, he was merely a nuisance, a tactless fool who was determined to put his foot in it. It was Gollancz's 'curious indiscretion' again. To reveal that the Communists were imposing an authoritarian rule over the cluster of Left-wing forces, and doing it by denouncing and betraying men who had fought and suffered in the anti-Fascist cause, was to let the wrong cat out of the bag. To tell the inconvenient truth about Communist methods could only 'play into the hands of' the Fascists. So that Orwell, still weak and ill from his wound and shaken with rage and pity by the fate that had overtaken the men he loved and admired, was met by frustration and delaying-tactics when he tried to tell his story to

[1] Hugh Thomas in *The Spanish Civil War* (1963), pp. 454–5, thinks that Yezhov, the N.K.V.D. chief, may have intended to stage Moscow-type trials in Spain so as to purge P.O.U.M. members and all other anti-Stalinists. This was staved off by the heroism of Andrés Nin, the P.O.U.M. leader, who refused to sign a confession of his own guilt and an implication of others. He was murdered for his pains.

an English public. Gollancz would not take the book. He rejected it without reading it—before it was finished, even—on the strength of the fact that Orwell had been fighting with the anarchist militia, the P.O.U.M., rather than with an orthodox Communist outfit like the International Brigade. And when Orwell brought it out with another publisher, the more independent-minded Secker and Warburg, he had to endure such indignities as being lectured by V. S. Pritchett in the *New Statesman.* To Pritchett (and, doubtless, to his editor Kingsley Martin) Orwell's appetite for the unvarnished truth was 'perverse'.[1] Small wonder that in the months that followed, Orwell went through a bad crisis of depression and discouragement: not about himself, but about the society he was living in. I base this judgement not on anything that is established about his personal life, which for all I know was outwardly normal, but on the manifest despair and disgust that comes, as physically and concretely as a smell, from *Coming Up For Air*, his most depressing book, which was published in 1939 and therefore presumably written in 1938, during the aftermath of the Spanish experience.

III

The best way to see clearly the new dimension of horror and despair that came into Orwell's mind after the events of 1937–8 is to set two novels side by side: *Coming Up For Air*, written, as we saw, in the trough that followed his return from Catalonia, and *Keep the Aspidistra Flying* (1936), the last novel, though not the last book, he wrote before going there.

To take the earlier book first, *Keep the Aspidistra Flying* is not a good novel, a fact which Orwell very soon came to appreciate, though he remained firm in his (correct) judgement that *A Clergyman's Daughter* (1935) was 'even worse'. (*Burmese Days*, 1934, in some ways a better book than either of them, is not quite germane to our present discussion because of its specialized theme.) The faults of *Aspidistra* are many. Its style is nagging and repetitive. Its story is not well told, being clotted

[1] *New Statesman & Nation*, 30 April, 1938.

with great lumps of essay-material and moving its figures about like puppets. Its characterization is all too often two-dimensional. Ravelston, for instance, is the nice rich sensitive man, so everything he does and says has to be in complete consistency with this formula; he is a 'humour', but without the vitality that makes some humours (Holmes and Watson, for instance, or Welch in *Lucky Jim*) amusing to read about.

These faults can be tolerated in a book which offers so much that is vital and hard-hitting. A much more serious defect is that the whole story is blurred by what seems to be a fundamental indecision in the author's mind. It is very much a novel with a purpose; but *what* purpose? No one in his senses would demand that a novel should preach—but if it starts out with an evident *wish* to preach, we are entitled to ask that it should preach one sermon at a time and do so coherently.

For about the first half of the book, the theme seems to be the familiar one of the artist struggling to be fertile in a sterilizing money-society. Gordon, wishing to develop his gifts as a poet, has thrown up a well-paid but shame-making job with an advertising agency and taken work as a bookseller's assistant. The idea is to get free of the poisoned air of competitive money-making and then let his imagination shape something beautiful. The trouble is that, amid the shabby-genteel miseries of his existence, his imagination switches itself off. In the limbo represented by Mr McKechnie's bookshop and Mrs Wisbeach's boarding-house, he is like a wraith between two worlds. If he were still in advertising he would at least have money and pleasant surroundings; if he were poor enough to sink into the slums, his life would at least be free of dreary respectability and the battle for 'appearances'. Rosemary, who tells him with evident sincerity that she loves him, has never become his mistress, and he cannot even make a whole-hearted play for her because Mrs Wisbeach will not have 'young women' in the house.

Stalemated as he is, Gordon must move, if anything is to happen in the story one way or the other. The novel fails because Orwell cannot, in the last analysis, make up his mind which way to move him. It looks, for a time, as if he had decided to push

Gordon decisively *downwards.* After a drunken spree in which he disgraces himself and loses his job, Gordon gets a similar job at a much lower level; he takes a room in a real slum, gives up all social and intellectual pretensions, and frankly accepts himself for what he is—a drop-out. Here Orwell was at a cross-roads. If he had decided to make Gordon Comstock a real artist, a poet of genuine power, the novel could have finished strongly on his self-recovery. Away from the aspidistra of mincing respectability, down among the frowzy freedom of bugs and the bailiffs, he might have written a handful of great sonnets. What he actually does is to seduce Rosemary, more or less absent-mindedly, get her with child, and then suddenly realize that *this*, for him, is the positive path. Marriage, responsibility, children, and back to the advertising agency.

This, too, might have made a strong finish, but as the book actually stands it does not. There is a muted, half-hearted quality about it, as if Orwell, while wishing Gordon Comstock well in his new life of fatherhood and office hours, feels regret at having to shrug off all the tirades in the first half of the book. All that splendid denunciation of the money-world, the swindle of advertising, the slow choking to death of an acquisitive society—and then Gordon, in the end, decides that it is humanly preferable to join that world rather than lick it! Will a life spent in making up advertising slogans to unload fake products on to the public really be better than working in the bookshop and trying to write poems? Well, but there is the embryo in Rosemary's womb, proof at last that 'once again, things were happening in the Comstock family'. With that, we have to be content. But we can't be content. It is not stated strongly or lyrically enough.

The failure is interesting because, like most failures, it is symptomatic. Orwell really was undecided on this point. On the one hand, he disliked the type who makes 'artistic' pretensions a licence for selfishness and irresponsibility. He very much preferred 'ordinary' people, who had jobs and families and paid their debts, to 'Bohemians' who were above such trivialities. Indeed, his references to the literary and artistic fringe of society, where Bohemians are to be met with, are always venomously hostile. 'Shrieking poseurs', 'verminous little lions'—such expressions abound. On the other hand, as he could not help being aware, there *have*, now and again, been real artists who have lived a shiftless life, without any money except what they cadged from friends and usually spent on drink, who have in the end repaid everything by producing great work. Just as there have been real artists who, without being Bohemian, have sunk below the level of respectable shabbiness into genuine, proletarian poverty, and found its climate fertilizing to their work. When William Faulkner was short of money, in 1929, he took a job shovelling coke at the town power-station of Oxford, Mississippi, and wrote *As I Lay Dying* during the slack period of midnight to 4 a.m., improvising a writing-desk from a wheelbarrow.

Orwell did not allow Gordon Comstock to come up this way. He did not, that is to say, allow him to be a genuine artist. And of course, if he were not a genuine artist, if his were merely the kind of half-baked talent that produces a slim volume and then dies a quiet death, then a job and marriage and fatherhood were, for him, the proper way back to self-respect. But what if he *had* been a genuine artist? Well, then, *Aspidistra* would have been a different book. And, I think, a more interesting one. For among the problems that Orwell never got round to solving was the problem of the artist; what kind of life he should be allowed to live, how much special privilege he should be allowed, whether he should be encouraged to think of himself as 'altogether exceptional' ('Benefit of Clergy') or to keep his feet on the ordinary earth.

Orwell's mind was never made up. All that *Aspidistra* really succeeds in saying is that if Gordon had had plenty of money, his lack of real talent would not have prevented his making a reputation as a poet and being lionized in literary *salons.* Which is true enough. And also that, since he did not possess the poetic gift of a Baudelaire, the best thing for him was to straighten up and fly right. Which again is true enough. But the story seems trivial when it is set against the lurid back-projection of a dying civilization. The book's vitality comes from Orwell's passionate rejection of capitalist society, 1934 model. The background is stronger than the foreground, if only because we cannot believe that Gordon Comstock would have been worth bothering about even if he had lived in an age of flourishing art and high civilization.

It is evident that the state of mind that produced the ending of *Aspidistra* was still very much with Orwell a few months later, when he wrote his review of Cyril Connolly's *The Rock Pool* in the *New English Weekly* of 23 July 1936. He finds fault with Connolly for his choice of subject-matter, the adventures of a young would-be writer who is sucked into 'one of those dreadful colonies of expatriates calling themselves artists that were dotted all over France in the late nineteen-twenties'. He goes on:

even to want to write about so-called artists who spend on sodomy what they have gained by sponging betrays a kind of spiritual inadequacy. For it is clear that Mr Connolly rather admires the disgusting beasts he depicts, and certainly he prefers them to the polite and sheeplike Englishman; he even compares them, in their ceaseless war against decency, to heroic savage tribes struggling against western civilisation. But this, you see, only amounts to a distaste for normal life and common decency, and one might equally well express it, as so many do, by scuttling beneath the moulting wing of Mother Church. Obviously, modern mechanized life becomes dreary if you let it. The awful thraldom of money is upon everyone and there are only three immediately obvious escapes. One is religion, another is unending work, the third is the kind of sluttish antinomianism—lying in bed till four in the afternoon, drinking Pernod—that Mr Connolly seems to admire. The third is certainly the worst, but in any case the essential evil is to think in terms of *escape*. The fact to which we have got to cling, as to a life-belt, is that it *is* possible to be a normal decent person and yet to be fully alive.

This is the Orwell who has some faith left, some hope that the day-to-day quality of life, even in a rotting society, would be tolerable because the decency of ordinary people would make it tolerable. He condemned 'escape' just as the orthodox Communists condemned it, though from a different point of view; by 'escape' they meant refusal to toe the Party line, whereas to him 'escape' could take a number of forms—of which, indeed, such line-toeing was one. He was, at this time, prepared to advocate a whole-hearted policy of involvement in everyday living. Fittingly, it was in this year that he married Eileen O'Shaughnessy, who is said to be the original of Rosemary in *Aspidistra*, and took her to live in the little general store he was running in a Hertfordshire village.

But other doubts stirred in his mind, as one can see from the very respectful assessment of Henry Miller which came four years later, in the essay 'Inside the Whale'. Orwell's account of Miller begins by praising him for making just that same descent into real poverty that Gordon Comstock made without effect. Miller is writing about the literary and artistic world of Paris, 'but he is dealing only with the under side of it, the lumpen-proletarian fringe which has been able to survive the slump because it is composed partly of genuine artists and partly of genuine scoundrels'. This seems to be a revealing sentence, admitting as it does that if the genuine scoundrel is not swept away by the crash of the Stock Market and the disappearance of *rentier* incomes, neither is the genuine artist. In other words, Gordon Comstock was neither.

The central issue of *Aspidistra*, then, insofar as we reach it through the story's main character, is blurred. The foundation of thinking and feeling in which Orwell embedded this issue, however, is very clear. His targets are very much what they remained for the next year or so, during the writing of *The Road to Wigan Pier*. It is the heartlessness, witlessness and gutlessness of a money-society, as seen by someone whose experience of that society has been sited mainly, though not exclusively, on the underside of the upper crust, among the people whose gentility makes them unfit to join in the scramble and sweat of everyday working life while not providing them with the means to rise definitely above it.

This society, as Orwell sees it in the novel, is undermined and threatened. It cannot survive—does not deserve to, indeed. On the other hand, the enemy that threatens it is only partly identified. There is, of course, the overhanging threat of war, which makes itself felt in the first chapter when Gordon gazes out of the bookshop window and imagines the drone of bombing-planes —'a sound which, at that moment, he passionately wanted to hear'. The death-wish of a stale and unjust society is caught in that phrase. But the nightmare is still in the present rather than the future. The stench arises from the habit-ridden, crumbling society, phosphorescent with decay, that is capitalism in its final stage. And at the end, when Gordon has found his positive aims in life, the whole question of what will happen to that life is quietly shelved.

Turn now to *Coming Up For Air.* This again is not a success in novelistic terms. George Bowling, the fat and rather beery-minded *homme moyen sensuel*, is made to voice Orwell's opinions a little too directly. A man like Bowling in actual life might very well agree with Orwell on most essentials, but he would be unlikely to express his views in such an Orwellian way. His voice would come to us, so to speak, through a layer of fat. Once again the vitality of the book is to be found in its hinterland, in the wide-angle view of Western capitalist society it presents to us.

In his short but extremely penetrating essay on *Helen's Babies* (1946), Orwell says that nineteenth-century America was fortunate in being 'a rich, empty country which lay outside the main stream of world events, and in which the twin nightmares that beset nearly every modern man, the nightmare of unemployment and the nightmare of State interference, had hardly come into being'. In *Aspidistra*, the first of these nightmares is vivid and actual: everybody fears the sack, hankers for more money and security; cringes to the boss. But only to the boss at work, the economic boss. The Commissar, 'half-gangster, half-gramophone', is not yet on the scene. To that extent the world of George Bowling is worse—colder, crueller, more inescapable—than the world of Gordon Comstock. When Bowling thinks of the future, he fears not only the ever-present financial insecurity, the endless work, work, work with the gutter only a few steps away; he fears also the new breed of tyrants, the myrmidons of totalitarianism, the leader and his strong-arm boys. Visiting his public-school-Oxford-classically-educated friend, Porteous (a figure who belongs much more naturally to Orwell's background than to George Bowling's), he reflects:

Old Porteous's mind, I thought, probably stopped working at about the time of the Russo-Japanese war. And it's a ghastly thing that nearly all the decent people, the people who *don't* want to go round smashing faces in with spanners, are like that. They're decent, but their minds have stopped. They can't defend themselves against what's coming to them, because they can't see it, even when it's under their noses. They think that England will never change and that England's the whole world. Can't grasp that it's just a left-over, a tiny corner that the bombs happen to have missed. But what about the new kind of men from eastern Europe, the stream-lined men who think in slogans and talk in bullets? They're on our track. Not long before they catch up with us. No Marquess of Queensberry rules for those boys. And all the decent people are paralyzed. Dead men and live gorillas. Doesn't seem to be anything between.

Bowling is caught between the dead past (which, like Orwell, he loves as much as any of its professional defenders) and the all too menacingly alive future. In between, there is a third region of nightmare. It concerns what we have since learnt to call 'the environment'. Part of Bowling's despair comes from the fact that he lives in a smirched, scribbled-over, cheapened England.

Once again we can take a perspective from 1946. In one of his *Tribune* pieces of that year, 'Thoughts on the Common Toad', Orwell pulls himself up after an entrancing description of the toad and its habits at various stages of the yearly cycle, and asks:

Is it wicked to take a pleasure in spring and other seasonal changes? To put it more precisely, is it politically reprehensible, while we are all groaning, or at any rate ought to be groaning, under the shackles of the capitalist system, to point out that life is frequently more worth living because of a blackbird's song, a yellow elm tree in October, or some other natural phenomenon which does not cost money and does not have what the editors of left-wing newspapers call a class angle? There is no doubt that many people think so. I know by experience that a favourable reference to 'Nature' in one of my articles is liable to bring me abusive letters, and though the key-word in these letters is usually 'sentimental', two ideas seem to be mixed up in them. One is that any pleasure in the actual process of life encourages a sort of political quietism. People, so the thought runs, ought to be discontented, and it is our job to multiply our wants and not simply to increase our enjoyment of the things we have already. The other idea is that this is the age of machines and that to dislike the machine, or even to want to limit its domination, is backward-looking, reactionary and slightly ridiculous. This is often backed up by the statement that a love of Nature is a foible of urbanized people who have no notion what Nature is really like. Those who really have to deal with the soil, so it is argued, do not love the soil, and do not take the faintest interest in birds or flowers, except from a strictly utilitarian point of view. To love the country one must live in the town, merely taking an occasional week-end ramble at the warmer times of year.

This last idea is demonstrably false. Medieval literature, for instance, including the popular ballads, is full of an almost Georgian enthusiasm for Nature, and the art of agricultural peoples such as the Chinese and Japanese centres always round trees, birds, flowers, rivers, mountains. The other idea seems to me to be wrong in a subtler way. Certainly we ought to be discontented, we ought not to simply find out ways of making the best of a bad job, and yet if we kill all pleasure in the actual process of life, what sort of future are we preparing for ourselves? If a man cannot enjoy the return of spring, why should he be happy in a labour-saving Utopia? What will he do with the leisure that the machine will give him? I have always suspected that if our economic and political problems are ever really solved, life will become simpler instead of more complex, and that the sort of pleasure one gets from finding the first primrose will loom larger than the sort of pleasure one gets from eating an ice to the tune of a Wurlitzer. I think that by retaining one's childhood love of such things as trees, fishes, butterflies and—to return to my first instance—toads, one makes a peaceful and decent future a little more probable, and that by preaching the doctrine that nothing is to be admired except steel and concrete, one merely makes it a little surer that human beings will have no outlet for their surplus energy except in hatred and leader worship.

What makes *Coming Up For Air* so peculiarly bitter to the taste is that, in addition to calling up the twin spectres of totalitarianism on the one hand and workless poverty on the other, it also declares the impossibility of 'retaining one's childhood love of such things as trees, fishes, butterflies', and so forth—because it postulates a world in which these things are simply not there any more.

This essay is written for people who are already acquainted with Orwell's books, more or less, and so there is no need to recount the plot of *Coming Up For Air.* Everyone who has even glanced through it will remember the remorseless way in which the forty-five-year-old insurance salesman, sneaking away from his semi in the suburbs to go back to his country boyhood at Lower Binfield in the Thames Valley, is dragged through one miry ditch of disappointment after another. The town has been swamped in raw red brick, the river has been polluted, the trees have been cut down, the house where he grew up is now Wendy's Tea-Shop, and so on through a grisly catalogue that would almost convict Orwell of exaggeration if it were not so manifestly a true account of what has happened to virtually the whole of South-east England. For two days Bowling wanders about, suffering. But one inner sanctuary remains. 'The pool at Binfield House', a deep, dark pond accessible only by those adventurous enough to trespass and hardy enough to tear themselves on thorn-bushes, that pool where he had lain in wait for enormous fish and which had remained through the years the node of his most powerful fantasies—it might, just *might*, be still there. Of course, the reader knows the kind of thing that is coming. In such a pitiless novel, a harmless fat man will not be left with his crumb of happiness *à la recherche du temps perdu.* There is a new, superior housing estate. The pond has been drained and used for a rubbish dump. Standing nearby is a simple-lifer, the kind of person Orwell had attacked in the closing chapters of *The Road to Wigan Pier* :

He began to show me around the estate. There was nothing left of the woods. It was all houses, houses—and what houses! Do you know these faked-up Tudor houses with the curly roofs and the buttresses that don't buttress anything, and the rock-gardens with concrete bird-baths and those red plaster elves you can buy at the florist's? You could see in your mind's eye the awful gang of food-cranks and spook-hunters and simple-lifers with £1000 a year that lived there. Even the pavements were crazy. I didn't let him take me far. Some of the houses made me wish I'd got a hand-grenade in my pocket. I tried to dump him down by asking whether people didn't object to living so near the lunatic asylum, but it didn't have much effect. Finally I stopped and said:

'There used to be another pool, besides the big one. It can't be far from here.'

'Another pool? Oh, surely not. I don't think there was ever another pool.'

'They may have drained it off,' I said. 'It was a pretty deep pool. It would leave a big pit behind.'

For the first time he looked a bit uneasy. He rubbed his nose.

'Oh-ah. Of course, you must understand our life up here is in some ways primitive. The simple life, you know. We prefer it so. But being so far from the town has its inconveniences, of course. Some of our sanitary arrangements are not altogether satisfactory. The dust-cart only calls once a month, I believe.'

'You mean they've turned the pool into a rubbish-dump?'

'Well, there *is* something in the nature of a ———' he shied at the word rubbish-dump. 'We have to dispose of tins and so forth, of course. Over there, behind that clump of trees.'

We went across there. They'd left a few trees to hide it. But yes, there it was. It was my pool, all right. They'd drained the water off. It made a great round hole, like an enormous well, twenty or thirty feet deep. Already it was half full of tin cans.

I stood looking down at the tin cans.

'It's a pity they drained it,' I said. 'There used to be some big fish in that pool.'

IV

We can, it seems to me, trace the temperature-chart of Orwell's thoughts and feelings after this fashion:

1910–1927: the normal rebellious feelings of a spirited and

intelligent schoolboy, forced against his will into an obsolete pattern of governing-class values in an unjust world.

1927–1937: bitter disgust with the state of the world, particularly that part of it about which he could speak from experience; sense of living 'in the wreck of a civilization', wrecked by industrialism with its ugliness and capitalism with its greed. These feelings tempered, but not very strongly and not consistently, by a feeling that 'socialism' was capable of building a better world.

1937–1940: subsidence into a state very close to total despair, after the snuffing-out of the hope that had flared briefly in revolutionary Catalonia. The realization (in Spain) that the Left was too split, and too sheep-like in its acceptance of totalitarian methods, to do any effective good in the world; realization (in England) that the propaganda-machine was already strong enough to drown individual honest testimony.

1940–1950: a rallying of the spirits caused partly by the fact that action, however painful, is better than waiting for action, and partly by the winning of the war.

Of the four phases I postulate here, only the last seems to me to need any comment. My evidence for saying that Orwell's spirits rose during the war years is concrete, but it is also vast and diffused—the kind of thing that gets referred to in indexes as 'passim'. It is partly a matter of tone. Overworked as he was, tied down to city life when he longed for the country, squandering his time on routine trivialities, underfed, far from healthy, Orwell nevertheless turned out a string of brilliant critical essays, from 'Inside the Whale' to 'Benefit of Clergy', which have a crackle of intellectual energy, a sharpness of observation and wit, and a sinewy strength of expression which would have been beyond the range of a man weighed down by despair. At the beginning of this period, in the essays on Dickens and *The Magnet* and Henry Miller, this buoyancy might have been the kind that Yeats described in 'Lapis Lazuli', the freedom from worry that comes with the realization that the jig is up, the tragic liberation from mere everyday unhappiness that Yeats hits off in the line, 'Hamlet and Lear are gay'. For these essays were finished, or almost finished, by the time the fighting actually started. But the same note is there in the essays on Wells, Kipling, comic postcards, and the rest. And the conclusive evidence builds up in the four-volume collection of miscellanea edited by Sonia Orwell and Ian Angus. That collection suffers necessarily from imbalance; of the four volumes, only the first is pre-war, and already with volume two we are in the world of rationing, the Blitz, the war-news and the casualty-lists. Even so, I think that anyone who reads steadily through the collection will see a lift in tone after volume one, and especially the latter part of that volume.

There are many reasons why this should be so. During those years, the war was fought and won, and this in itself was an enormous fact in Orwell's experience. He identified himself totally with the fight to rid the earth of Fascism; indeed, the urge to contribute his all in the way of effort and sacrifice led him first to try to get into the Army although he was obviously quite unfit, and later to underfeed himself and his wife in the hope that if they did not take up their full rations there would be more for other people. (Considering what the rations were, and that they had been worked out scrupulously on the basis of the number of mouths to feed, this decision was evidently an emotional compulsion rather than a responsible policy. It probably led to his wife's death under the anaesthetic for a minor operation in 1945.) He despised the pacifist wing of the intelligentsia for taking the attitude that war, any war, was merely a squalid mistake and that it made no difference who won. When invasion seemed imminent, in 1940, he refused to take the advice of those who wanted him to go to Canada 'in order to stay alive and keep up propaganda', on the grounds that 'even as propaganda, one's death might achieve more than going abroad and living more or less unwanted on other people's charity'.

Hitler and the Gestapo were defeated, even at the cost of strengthening Stalin and the N.K.V.D., and what was more they were defeated largely by the persistence and courage of Orwell's beloved 'common man'. So the long years of bread-and-marge, the sickly aspidistra behind the yellow lace curtains, the rat-like scurry of the clerks swarming into the Underground twice a day, had not broken England's spirit after all. Even the higher-ups had redeemed themselves to some extent, for, as Orwell noted in *The Lion and the Unicorn* in 1941 :

One thing that has always shown that the English ruling class are *morally* fairly sound, is that in time of war they are ready enough to get themselves killed. Several dukes, earls and what-nots were killed in the recent campaign in Flanders. This could not happen if these people were the cynical scoundrels they are sometimes declared to be.

Another thing that cheered Orwell during the war years was the perceptible shift of English life towards a Socialist atmosphere. This was partly a matter of the surface (at a time when it was unpatriotic to grab too many consumer goods, wealth could not advertize itself by 'conspicuous consumption'), but partly, also, a realization, deep in the bones of the nation, that at the end of the years of battle there must be a new social deal. Orwell, for his part, spent the first year or two of the war in expectation of a revolution; not the kind of revolution which meant fighting in the streets, for *that* kind of disruption would have let the Germans in immediately, but a silent, peaceful revolution through economic and social measures. He expected it because he did not believe that a capitalist England would have the moral health and the physical courage to fight the war. Later, he was to confess in one of his London Letters to the *Partisan Review* that he had been mistaken; ramshackle old England had managed to come through the war without actually revolutionizing her social system. Still, a change of mood there had been; in 1945, the social revolution did actually come; and Orwell found the air much more breathable from 1940 onwards. To quote again from *The Lion and the Unicorn* :

Hitler will at any rate go down in history as the man who made the City of London laugh on the wrong side of its face. For the first time in their lives the comfortable were uncomfortable, the professional optimists had to admit that there was something wrong. It was a great step forward. From that time onwards the ghastly job of trying to convince artificially stupefied people that a planned economy might be better that a free-for-all in which the worst man wins—that job will never be quite so ghastly again.

I would claim, then, that during the last decade of his life Orwell emerged from despair. Of course he still found much wrong with the world. Of course, as a writer, he still functioned mainly as a satirist. But one thinks of him as he himself thought of Dickens—'a man who is always fighting against something, but who fights in the open and is not frightened'. Even his two anti-totalitarian satires, nightmarish as they may be, are not so much expressions of despair as missiles aimed at definite targets. Despair, essentially, has a core of inertia running through it. Orwell's final satires are not inert, and to that extent they are not despairing. *Animal Farm* is like a grenade thrown straight into the ammunition dump during some daring guerrilla raid. And even *1984*, more deeply tinged with loathing and more clearly the work of a dying man, shows Orwell using his last strength to strike a blow for what he loved against what he hated. 'Pessimistic' it may be, but to the extent that it is sharply motivated it is constructive. It is not 'the sickness unto death'.

In the nineteen-thirties, however, Orwell came close to that sickness. He saw democracy, rotted inwardly by the poison of greed and irresponsibility, facing a ruthless totalitarianism sworn to destroy it. The Spanish effort had failed, and with it had gone —as he could not help but believe—the last hope that men of goodwill might co-operate to save the world. He was prepared to sell his life dearly, but he had, I think, no hope.

Naturally I am not such a complacent fool as to make it a point *against* Orwell that he experienced despair as the thirties ebbed away. That decade had seen so many lights go out, and the new ones that were to offer our present gleams of hope were as yet so far in the future, that any man who combined imagination with decency would find that, together, they added up to despair. Orwell's own image for the thirties was 'a riot of appalling folly that suddenly becomes a nightmare, a scenic railway ending in a torture-chamber'. In such a situation, despair can be the only honourable reaction. Such, at any rate, was the view taken by E. M. Forster, who remarked almost parenthetically, in a book review in the *New Statesman & Nation* of 10 December 1938, that 'there is nothing disgraceful about despair. In 1938–39, the more despair a man can take on board without sinking, the more completely he is alive'.

Orwell never sank under his load of despair. But it must have been, at times, a near thing. His work abounds in passages—usually thrown off, like Forster's remark quoted above, more or less by the way—which reveal an intimate knowledge of suffering and self-doubt. The road from depression to cold war was a long one for everyone, but it must have been specially long for him, with his capacity to identify with suffering and to feel it in his own blood and bones.

As I write, it is once more the fashion to decry Orwell, as it was in the thirties. Now as then, his truth-telling is dismissed as 'perverse', and his warnings are shrugged off by what he himself called 'the huge tribe known as "the right left people"'. Now, as then, the most vicious digs at Orwell come from men whose basic intellectual position is totalitarian, the sort of people who are always ready to point out the flaws in an untidy democracy, but would see nothing disturbing in the dreadful tidiness of, say, a classroom of North Vietnamese children speaking in unison, 'No one loves Uncle Ho more than the children!' We are plagued with these people now, as we were in the thirties, and for much the same reasons.

It is a testimony to the continuing vitality of Orwell's work that totalitarian-minded critics hate him so much. They hate him because he is a thorn in their flesh. May he stay there for ever.

'To write for my own race': Notes on the Fiction of Flann O'Brien

ONE sunlit day in 1946, or it may have been 1947, I went into the Eagle and Child public house in Oxford, and found Kingsley Amis turning over the leaves of a book and chuckling continuously. 'Philip lent me this,' he said, showing it to me. Since we both (and quite rightly) accepted Philip Larkin as the supreme arbiter on literary matters, this attracted my interest at once. I looked at the book: *At Swim-Two-Birds*, by Flann O'Brien. Neither title nor author meant anything to me; I did not know that Swim-Two-Birds (or Swim-Two-Ducks) was a literal translation of an Irish place-name, nor that 'Flann O'Brien' was one of the two pseudonyms of a Dublin writer named Brian O'Nolan —the other being Myles na gCopaleen, under which name he wrote a regular satirical column for the *Irish Times.*

I borrowed the book, whether or not with the permission of the absent owner I do not now recollect, and swallowed it in huge gulps. At once, it went straight into my bloodstream. It had been published in 1939, not a good moment for the appearance in England of any book, least of all a book from Ireland, and it seemed to have sunk without trace. In the next ten years I met fewer than a score of people who had read it. But these readers tended to form a secret society, they worked underground, and finally another publisher re-issued the book in 1960, this time to an adequate if not altogether perceptive critical reception.

To attempt a criticism of *At Swim-Two-Birds* is a task I have alternately longed and dreaded to approach. I love it and have always been willing to testify to my love. Yet to discuss it? To do anything more ambitious than merely assert its uniqueness? In an essay published in 1962 I made a passing reference to *At*

Swim-Two-Birds as 'a Gargantuan comic novel which makes a simultaneous exploration, on four or five levels, of Irish civilization'. The vagueness of 'four or five' suggests that I wasn't counting the levels very carefully or distinguishing them with much clarity, but what interests me now, looking back, is my untroubled assumption that the book explored 'Irish civilization'. I think so now and I thought so then, but why was I so certain? Partly, I think, for the very reason that it *was* so amusing. Funny writing never really comes over as funny unless it is saying something serious; wild humour in particular, unless it is anchored to the rocks, just floats up into the empyrean and vanishes in a cloud of boredom. As George Orwell noted in connection with Dickens, 'You can only create if you *care*. Types like Squeers and Micawber could not have been produced by a hack writer looking for something to be funny about.' O'Nolan was a desperately funny writer, therefore (I felt) his work must be about something. If it had merely been a romp, it would have been perfunctory and the perfunctoriness would have shown through.

Basically, *At Swim-Two-Birds* is about a man writing a story about a man writing a story. The narrator (he is nowhere named) is a young student, living with an uncle in Dublin on funds supplied by his father, who lives, presumably, in the country, in order to take his degree at the National University. The young man's life is described in tones of guarded flatness, drained of colour but tinged with irony. He spends a great deal of time in bed, meditating on life and art and in particular on 'my spare-time literary activities', as he calls the *magnum opus* he is slowly composing. The uncle is portrayed in comic-satirical vein, though without any real malice, as a lower-middle-class Dubliner, 'holder of Guinness clerkship the third class'. Through the sardonic eye of the narrator, we catch occasional glimpses of the uncle's life. He converses long and earnestly with his friend Mr Corcoran; he holds a meeting at his house for the purpose (it seems) of arranging a welcome for some local celebrity who is paying a visit home; we know of this episode only because the nephew comes in that evening the worse for drink and is co-opted into acting as secretary to the meeting, but it is used very skilfully to indicate the nature of the uncle's social circle, their prejudices and preoccupations. One of the men present tells a funny story against the Jesuits; another puts forward the suggestion that at the proposed *Ceilidhe* the programme should include an old-time waltz, and is strongly opposed by Mr Corcoran. 'A Ceilidhe is a Ceilidhe. I mean, we have our own. We have plenty of our own dances without crossing the road to borrow what we can't wear. See the point? It's all right but it's not for us. Leave the waltz to the jazz-boys. By God they're welcome to it as far as I'm concerned.' The refreshment budget is then discussed and it is decided to 'add another bottle and a couple of dozen stout'. The picture is thumb-nail size (but it is a vivid miniature of the mind and life of that generation of the Dublin petty *bourgeoisie* who would be, say, sixty in 1940: the men who remembered the fall of Parnell, who had been of fighting age at the time of the uprising of 1916. Narrow as they are, seen as they are through a comic lens, these men are given a stiff, provincial dignity that redeems them.

Then there is the life of the narrator himself. Obviously the decision to give him no name is a mild piece of symbolism. He is the writer, the viewing and recording lens, the youth who already, before tasting life, has waved aside the cup and chosen a contemplative role. He lies on his bed as much as possible, smoking and thinking; when he emerges, it is to go to a lecture at the University—another brilliant short sketch—or to consume pints of 'plain' (i.e. porter, a crude, dark form of draught stout) with his harmlessly disreputable acquaintances. The flavour of these excursions is fairly suggested by the following extract:

As I exchanged an eye-message with Brinsley, a wheezing beggar inserted his person at my side and said :

'Buy a scapular or a stud, Sir.'

This interruption I did not understand. Afterwards, near Lad Lane police station a small man in black fell in with us and tapping me often about the chest, talked to me earnestly on the subject of Rousseau, a member of the French nation. He was animated, his pale features striking in the starlight and his voice going up and falling in the lilt of his argumentum. I did not understand his talk and was personally unacquainted with him. But Kelly was taking in all he said, for he stood near him, his taller head inclined in an attitude of close attention. Kelly then made a low noise and opened his mouth and covered the small man from shoulder to knee with a coating of unpleasant buff-coloured puke. Many other things happened on that night now imperfectly recorded in my memory but that incident is still very clear to me in my mind. Afterwards the small man was some distance from us in the lane, shaking his divested coat and rubbing it along the wall. He is a little man that the name of Rousseau will always recall to me. Conclusion of reminiscence.

The narrator also attends, on at least one occasion, an evening of high-minded literary talk at the house of a man called Byrne. In his mild way, he is anxious to shine in this circle and gives an account of the progress of his novel 'in order to amuse them and win their polite praise'.

This novel is a full-blown work of experimentation. The narrator has, of course, an elaborate theory of the art of fiction, which he expounds in a conversation with his friend Brinsley.

In reply to an inquiry, it was explained that a satisfactory novel should be a self-evident sham to which the reader could regulate at will the degree of his credulity. It was undemocratic to compel characters to be uniformly good or bad or poor or rich. Each should be allowed a private life, self-determination and a decent standard of living. This would make for self-respect, contentment and better service. It would be incorrect to say that it would lead to chaos. Characters should be interchangeable as between one book and another. The entire corpus of existing literature should be regarded as a limbo from which discerning authors could draw their characters as required, creating only when they failed to find a suitable existing puppet. The modern novel should be largely a work of reference. Most authors could spend their time saying what has been said before—usually said much better. A wealth of references to existing works would acquaint the reader instantaneously with the nature of each character, would obviate tiresome explanations and would effectively preclude mountebanks, upstarts, thimbleriggers and persons of inferior education from an understanding of contemporary literature. Conclusion of explanation.

That is all my bum, said Brinsley.

This programme, absurd as it is, comes reasonably close to describing the literary method of *At Swim-Two-Birds.* In particular, it covers the nonchalant non-credibility of the story ('a self-evident sham'), the autonomy and indeed rebelliousness of the imaginary personnel, and the frequent resort to borrowing of characters from previous writing or from legend. Except that true to the book's sardonic farcical atmosphere, the 'previous writing' turns out to be itself an invention, and the legends highly fantasticated.

The narrator's novel is about a man named Dermot Trellis, a writer, who lives at the Red Swan Hotel and has spent the last twenty years entirely in bed, rising only to supervise the washing of his linen by a servant-girl, Teresa. Trellis's object is to write a highly moral work on the dangers of vice and wickedness, and for this reason he creates a villain, named Furriskey, who is to exemplify the lusts of the flesh, low cunning and malevolence of every description. Furriskey's first task is to entrap and dishonour a respectable working girl. In the event, when the couple meet they fall in love and decide to form a regular and happy union. This they are able to do only when Trellis is asleep; when awake, he forces all his characters to live with him at the Red Swan Hotel and keeps them under strict surveillance.

Trellis has also created two other men, Shanahan and Lamont. Shanahan is present merely to provide a confidant for Furriskey, but Lamont's function in the plot is that he is the brother of Sheila Lamont, a high-minded and beautiful girl whom Furriskey will also debauch; Lamont will then challenge him. Miss Lamont is also provided with a father in the person of the legendary hero Finn Mac Cool.

Right from the start, things go wrong. Shanahan administers drugs to Trellis to keep him asleep most of the time, and the characters can thus get on with living their own lives. Furriskey marries the girl and they settle down to cosy domestic happiness, except when Trellis briefly awakes and they have to hurry over to the Red Swan Hotel. Trellis, during one of his rare spells of activity, creates Sheila Lamont and then falls in love with her and ravishes her himself, so that she becomes pregnant. Two characters looted by Trellis from folklore are thereby brought into the action; the Pooka MacPhellimey (no doubt MacPhellimey is an individual but the Pooka is a well-identified kind of Irish devil, related to the Welsh *pwcca*, Shakespeare's Puck, etc.), and the Good Fairy. These two are to bargain, in traditional fashion, for ascendancy over the soul of Miss Lamont's unborn child.

As it happens, Miss Lamont never appears in the story; she dies at the birth of her child, who bears the name Orlick Trellis. The *accouchement* provides the occasion for a roll-call of the characters, who by this time are more numerous than this résumé would suggest. Finn Mac Cool, as well as being a hero in his own right, is also a bard with an extensive repertory of ancient Irish legends. Scarcely heeded by the other characters, who regard his tales as respectable but quite irrelevant to their own lives, he provides a continual ground-base to the novel by recounting the saga of the mad King Sweeney.

There are in this narrative of Finn's a good many things that go over the head of a reader like myself who knows virtually nothing of ancient Irish literature. On the other hand, anyone who has ever looked into the literature of the Middle Ages at all, in any language, can see that another layer of parody is being added to the structure, and that in the main it is affectionate parody. We first meet Finn in a fairly long passage near the beginning of the book, when he is shown as discoursing before a traditional audience of his own people, ritually prompted to speech and song by a person named Conan whose presence is left unexplained, but who is constantly at hand ('hidden Conan') whenever Finn is reciting. In this passage, Finn gives a preliminary indication of the kind of matter that interests him and the Ireland he represents, and the passage concludes with a kind of lament.

Melodious is your voice, said Conan.

Small wonder, said Finn, that Finn is without honour in the breast of a sea-blue book, Finn that is twisted and trampled and tortured for the weaving of a story-teller's book-web. Who but a book-poet would dishonour the God-big Finn for the sake of a gap-worded story? Who could have the saint Ceallach carried off by his four acolytes and he feeble and thin from his Lent-fast, laid in the timbers of an old boat, hidden for a night in a hollow oak tree and slaughtered without mercy in the morning, his shrivelled body to be torn by a wolf and a scaldcrow and the Kite of Cluain-Eo? Who could think to turn the children of a king into white swans with the loss of their own bodies, to be swimming the two seas of Erin in snow and ice-cold rain without bards or chess-boards, without their own tongues for discoursing melodious Irish, changing the fat white legs of a maiden into plumes and troubling her body with shameful eggs? Who could put a terrible madness on the head of Sweeney for the slaughter of a single Lent-gaunt cleric, to make him live in tree-tops and roost in the middle of a yew, not a wattle to the shielding of his mad head in the middle of the wet winter, perished to the marrow without company of women or strains of harp-pluck, with no feeding but stag-food and the green branches? Who but a story-teller? Indeed, it is true that there has been ill-usage to the men of Erin from the book-poets of the world and dishonour to Finn, with no knowing the nearness of disgrace or the sorrow of death, or the hour when they may swim for swans or trot for ponies or bell for stags or croak for frogs or fester for the wounds on a man's back.

True for telling, said Conan.

We shall revert to this lament later on. What concerns us at the moment is the anticipatory reference to the madness of Sweeney. King Sweeney assaulted the pious hermit Ronan, who was at that moment in the act of taping out the measurements of a new church; whereupon Ronan put a curse on Sweeney which caused him to run mad and naked, rather like Lear, across the length and breadth of Ireland. Sweeney's sufferings are described in Finn's narrative in a vein that mingles the farcical with the terrifying, and he comments on his own plight in a number of lyrics, some of which are mere comical parodies while others come across with genuine force as poems. For example:

A year to last night
I have lodged there in branches
from the flood-tide to the ebb-tide
naked.

Bereft of fine women-folk,
the brooklime for a brother—
our choice for a fresh meal
is watercress always.

Without accomplished musicians
without generous women,
no jewel-gift for bards—
respected Christ, it has perished me.

The thorntop that is not gentle
has reduced me, has pierced me,
it has brought me near death
the brown thorn-bush.

Once free, once gentle,
I am banished for ever,
wretch-wretched I have been
a year to last night.

Without going back to the envelope-story of the narrator and his uncle, we are now operating on at least three levels. The Pooka and the Good Fairy are pure folklore, rendered in terms of outright farce. Finn and his tale of Sweeney come from the ancient heroic world of Ireland.[1] Then we have Furriskey, Shanahan and Lamont, and Mrs Furriskey, who are modern Dubliners of a lower social class than are the narrator's uncle and his friends. Now we must take a step further. Shanahan, an older man, has worked in the past for a Dublin writer of sentimental Western romances (*Flower o' the Prairie*, etc.), an acquaintance of Trellis's called William Tracey. He is given to

[1] The title of the novel, incidentally, derives from this area of the story, since one of the places visited by Sweeney in his crazed wandering is 'the church at Snamh-da-en (or Swim-Two-Birds) by the side of the Shannon'.

reminiscing about the stories in which Tracey involved him, and in particular about two cowboys, Slug Willard and Shorty Andrews. In one of his tales, the three of them go off to another part of Dublin to recover some cattle rustled by a rival outfit, and finding the armed resistance too strong, go away and come back with the Dublin constabulary; we are finally given a police-court report of the affair from a local newspaper.

True to the manifesto which lays down that characters should not be created *ab ovo* except when there are no suitable ones already in existence, Furriskey comes to life in a room at the Red Swan Hotel and, wandering nervous and bewildered in this strange world, explores the house until he finds a room in which Shanahan and Lamont are waiting for him. They explain his duties, and he goes out to encounter the girl whom Trellis wishes him to deflower. On his melancholy return, he finds Shanahan and Lamont sitting by the fire, and now Finn is with them. The scene that follows brings into wild juxtaposition Finn's narrative of mad Sweeney and Shanahan's reminiscences of the old Tracey days: ancient, lofty Ireland and modern pulp-magazine culture are brought together in hopeless incomprehension. But Shanahan's lore extends beyond Westerns. He knows and admires the work of Jem Casey, the labouring poet.

It's a quare one and one that takes a lot of beating. Not a word to nobody, not a look to left or right but the brain-box going there all the time. Just Jem Casey, a poor ignorant labouring man but head and shoulders above the bloody lot of them, not a man in the whole country to beat him when it comes to getting together a bloody pome—not a poet in the whole world that could hold a candle to Jem Casey, not a man of them fit to stand beside him. By God I'd back him to win by a canter against the whole bloody lot of them give him his due.

Is that a fact, Mr Shanahan, said Lamont. It's not every day in the week you come across a man like that.

Do you know what I'm going to tell you, Mr Lamont, he was a man that could give the lot of them a good start, pickaxe and all. He was a man that could meet them . . . and meet the best . . . and beat them at their own game, now I'm telling you.

I suppose he could, said Furriskey.

Now I know what I'm talking about. Give a man his due. If a man's station is high or low he is all the same to the God I know. Take the bloody black hats off the whole bunch of them and where are you?

That's the way to look at it, of course, said Furriskey.

Give them a bloody pick, I mean, Mr Furriskey, give them the shaft of a shovel into their hand and tell them to dig a hole and have the length of a page of poetry off by heart in their heads before the five o'clock whistle. What will you get? By God you could take off your hat to what you'd get at five o'clock from the crowd and that's a sure sharkey.

You'd be wasting your time if you waited till five o'clock if you ask me, said Furriskey with a nod of complete agreement.

You're right there, said Shanahan, you'd be waiting around for bloody nothing. Oh I know them and I know my hard Casey too. By Janey he'd be up at the whistle with a pome a yard long, a bloody lovely thing that would send my nice men home in a hurry, home with their bloody tails between their legs. Yes, I've seen his pomes and read them and . . . do you know what I'm going to tell you, I have loved them.

A poem of Casey's is then solemnly recited: a piece of heavy doggerel with the refrain 'A PINT OF PLAIN IS YOUR ONLY MAN'. This poem provides the necessary contrast with the lyrics of Sweeney, and also hooks on to the enveloping story, in which one of the narrator's college friends, as they sit on high stools at a bar, utters the same refrain.

He leaned over and put his face close to me in an earnest manner.

Do you know what I am going to tell you, he said with his wry mouth, a pint of plain is your only man.

This scene is the first crescendo of the book, the first to illustrate the technique of superimposition and palimpsest which links this novel firmly with central twentieth-century works from *The Waste Land* and the *Cantos* to *Finnegan's Wake*. It is also the first passage in which the critique of Irish civilisation becomes explicit. Shanahan and Lamont, bored by Finn's recital and continually interrupting it, are contrasted with the audience he had in the earlier extract, hanging on his words and breaking their silence only in prescribed moments of antiphon.

This scene is the first of three set-pieces which make up the structure of the book's inner action, the story of Trellis and his characters. The second set-piece is the journey of the Pooka and the Good Fairy towards the birth-chamber of Orlick Trellis. The Good Fairy comes to the Pooka early in the morning, wakes him, gets into his pocket, and the two set off. In the course of their journey they meet the two Dublin cowboys, Slug Willard and Shorty Andrews; then Jem Casey; and finally mad King Sweeney. Crazed and enfeebled by his sufferings, Sweeney is helped to his feet by the others as if he were the victim of a street accident. The scene has a wild, farcical poignancy; it is like nothing else I can remember having read; there are, of course, similar effects in *Ulysses* but this scene, coming as it does after a long exposure to the book's multiple action, strikes me as more moving than the comparable passages in Joyce. The scene is too long to quote (it occurs on pages 179 to 185 in the MacGibbon & Kee edition of 1960) but here is a short specimen:

The madman fluttered his lids in the searchlight of the sun and muttered out his verses as he tottered hither and thither and back again backwards in the hold of his two keepers.

> Though my flittings are unnumbered,
> my clothing today is scarce,
> I personally maintain my watch
> on the tops of mountains.
>
> O fern, russet long one,
> your mantle has been reddened,
> there's no bedding for an outcast
> on your branching top.
>
> Nuts at terce and cress-leaves,
> fruits from an apple-wood at noon,
> a lying-down to lap chill water—
> your fingers torment my arms.

Put green moss in his mouth, said the Good Fairy querulously, are we going to spend the rest of our lives in this place listening to talk the like of that? There is a bad smell in this pocket, it is not doing me any good. What are you in the habit of keeping in it, Sir?

Nothing, replied the Pooka, but tabacca.

It's a queer smell for tabacca, said the Good Fairy.

One and sixpence I pay in silver coin for an ounce of it, said the Pooka, and nice as it is for the wee pipe, it is best eaten. It is what they call shag tabacca.

Notwithstanding all that, said the Good Fairy, there is a queer hum off it. It would be the price of you if I got sick here in your pocket.

Now be very careful, said the Pooka.

Quick march my hard man, said Casey briskly to the king, put your best leg forward and we will get you a bed before the sun goes down, we'll get a sup of whiskey into you to make you sleep.

We'll get you a jug of hot punch and a packet of cream crackers with plenty of butter, said Slug, if you'll only walk, if you'll only pull yourself together, man.

And getting around the invalid in a jabbering ring, they rubbed him and cajoled and coaxed, and plied him with honey-talk and long sweet-lilted sentences full of fine words, and promised him metheglin and mugs of viscous tar-black mead thickened with white yeast and the spoils from hives of mountain-bees, and corn-coarse nourishing farls of wheaten bread dipped in musk-scented liquors and sodden with Belgian sherry, an orchard and a swarm of furry honey-glutted bees and a bin of sun-bronzed grain from the granaries of the Orient in every drop as it dripped at the lifting of the hand to the mouth . . .

A long catalogue follows, doubtless in parody of ancient Irish heroic lays. There is nothing *new* in this; formally, it is only doing again what Eliot did when he brought Phlebas the Phoenician and Tiresias into juxtaposition with the typist putting a record on the gramophone, or Joyce when he equated Nausicaa with Gerty MacDowell. But it is, to my mind, at the very least the equal of these celebrated passages. It is so richly imagined, so concrete; it arises spontaneously from a sense of the irreconcilable elements in the Irish consciousness; we do not hear the click of scissors and the swish of the paste-brush, we see and participate.

Finally the Pooka's party arrive at the Red Swan Hotel, and while waiting for the birth and the subsequent refreshments they play cards. The Good Fairy loses, and having no money is obliged to raise a loan from the Pooka, who exacts the condition that the Good Fairy shall give up all claim to influence the child who is coming into the world. Orlick Trellis is thus born and nurtured into devilish cruelty and vengefulness. The Pooka takes him away to his cabin in the woods for a short intensive training period, at the end of which he makes his entry into everyday life as lodger at the house of Mr and Mrs Furriskey. There, Orlick reveals an inherited gift for writing, and it is decided by all the characters that he shall be the instrument of their revenge on Dermot Trellis by composing a counter-story in which Dermot is humiliated and destroyed. And the third set-piece is the narrative of Orlick Trellis, read to Furriskey, Lamont, and Shanahan.

Orlick is a consciously literary writer, dealing in fine phrases and subtle effects which naturally please his audience no better that the organ-music of Finn Mac Cool. They constantly interrupt him with demands for a short, crisp narrative in which Dermot Trellis meets a quick and unceremonious end. Orlick begins with an opening to the story that links Dermot Trellis decisively with King Sweeney; lying in bed in the early morning, he is disturbed by the ringing of a bell, and finds that a saintly cleric is taping out the measurements of a new church. The reader has barely time to note the parallel between the two suffering heroes, when the interruptions follow their familiar pattern.

What? said Trellis. Who did you say you were? What was that noise? What is the ringing for?

The bells of my acolyte, said the cleric. His voice was of a light quality and was unsupported by the majority of his wits, because these were occupied with the beauty of the round thing, its whiteness, its star-twinkle face.

My acolytes are in your garden. They are taping the wallsteads of a sunbright church and ringing their bells in the morning.

I beg your pardon, Sir, said Shanahan, but this is a bit too high up for us. This delay, I mean to say. The fancy stuff, couldn't you leave it out or make it short, Sir? Couldn't you give him a dose of something, give him a varicose vein in the bloody heart and get him out of that bed?

Orlick placed his pen in the centre of his upper lip and exerted a gentle pressure by a movement of his head or hand, or both, so that his lip was pushed upwards.

Result : baring of teeth and gum.

You overlook my artistry, he said. You cannot drop a man unless you first lift him. See the point?

Oh, there's that too, of course, said Shanahan.

Or a varicose vein across the scalp, said Furriskey, near the brain, you know. I believe that's the last.

I saw a thing in a picture once, said Shanahan, a concrete-mixer, you understand, Mr Orlick, and three of your men fall into it when it is working full blast, going like the hammers of hell.

The mixture to be taken three times after meals, Lamont said laughing.

You must have patience, gentlemen, counselled Orlick, the whiteness of a slim hand for warning.

A concrete-mixer, said Shanahan.

I'm after thinking of something good, something very good unless I'm very much mistaken, said Furriskey in an eager way, black in the labour of his fine thought. When you take our hero from the concrete-mixer, you put him on his back on the road and order full steam ahead with the steam-roller. . . .

Orlick begins again, still with the intention of having Trellis assault the cleric as Sweeney assaulted Ronan. But his audience will not accept the subject. ('You won't get very far by attacking the church.') He therefore makes a new start and brings in the Pooka MacPhelimey to haul Trellis out of bed and start him on a nightmare journey. From this point on, the parallel between Trellis and Sweeney is driven home. Their sufferings are described with the same blend of the horrific and the comical, and there are a number of verbal echoes which grapple the stories together.

At last Trellis is brought to trial, in a scene which reminds us both of Kafka and of the night-town section of *Ulysses* without ever swerving from its own individuality. The judges, a twelve-man board who also serve as jury, are made up of minor characters in Trellis's writings. The accusers range from William Tracey, author of *Flower o' the Prairie*, to a shorthorn cow who alleges that Trellis once caused her acute discomfort by neglecting to milk her. The trial inexorably grinds on, with the Pooka acting as clerk of the court, and Trellis is about to be taken out and executed when he is saved by an accident. Teresa, the servant back at the Red Swan Hotel, goes into his bedroom and, finding it empty, begins to tidy up and throws some sheets of paper from the floor on to the fire. These happen to be the sheets of Trellis's novel which bring Furriskey and company into being. At once the trial scene dissolves and Trellis, exhausted and frightened, is standing in the street outside his house. He knocks and Teresa comes down to admit him.

He was attired in his night-shirt, which was slightly discoloured as if by rain, and some dead leaves were attached to the soles of his poor feet. His eyes gleamed and he did not speak but walked past her in the direction of the stairs. He then turned and coughing slightly, stared at her and she stood there, the oil-lamp in her hand throwing strange shadows on her soft sullen face.

Ah, Teresa, he muttered.

Where were you in your night-shirt, Sir? she asked.

I am ill, Teresa, he murmured. I have done too much thinking and writing, too much work. My nerves are troubling me. I have bad nightmares and queer dreams and I walk when I am asleep. I am very tired. The doors should be locked.

You could easily get your death, Sir, Teresa said.

Without leaning on it too ponderously, it seems to me that Teresa is Ireland, in much the same way that the old woman who brings milk to the tower in the opening section of *Ulysses* is Ireland. Humble and unnoticed, with her 'soft sullen face' and her cheap clothes, she is the bedrock reality that underlies all the memories and the mental conflicts. Trellis's sufferings, like Sweeney's, are imposed on him by the power of the imagination; Sweeney is specifically described at the beginning of the book as exposed to dishonour and suffering by 'a story-teller', and Finn as 'twisted and trampled and tortured for the weaving of a story-teller's book-web'. Throughout the story, the imagination speaks unheeded; Shanahan and Lamont, with their repetitive, empty chatter, continually interrupt both Finn and Orlick, while the judges at Trellis's trial sit at a long bar with glasses of stout in their hands. The judgment of the saloon bar decides everything: is it fanciful to see in this an echo of the marrow-bone bitterness one finds in a poem like Yeats's—

> All day I'd looked in the face
> What I had thought 'twould be
> To write for my own race,
> And the reality . . .?

From this torment, Trellis is released by the simple action of a servant-girl who burns a few sheets of paper. And if Teresa, with her humble usefulness, saves Trellis, a similar *éclaircissement* happens in the enveloping narrative, where the nephew, having unexpectedly passed his examinations (a kind of trial with multiple judges) is greeted cordially by his uncle and Mr Corcoran and feels a releasing warmth towards them.

The imagination is wrong and leads to suffering: a simple art-free life is best. Am I trying to impose this crude moral on *At Swim-Two-Birds*? Most certainly not. But the book is about Ireland, and Ireland is a country where the dream, the imagined role and the struck attitude, have always bulked larger than the pebble and clod of reality. The Irish are a small nation, but wherever there is a theatre there are Irish actors, and their poets have always been among the greatest; and for this power of projecting images there is a price to be paid. Yeats, whose shrewdness matched his poetic intensity, put his finger on this danger when he wrote, in *Ireland after Parnell*, that 'No country could have more natural distaste for equality, for in every circle there was some man ridiculous for posing as the type of some romantic or distinguished trait.'

The man who lives by the imagination, who is haunted by great memories that cannot be reduced to order, who sees the world in the colours cast over it by his dreams and longings, is doomed to suffer as Trellis and Finn and Sweeney suffer. He will be plagued by the Pooka, or by characters he has dreamed into being, or taken over from the dreams of other men; and he will be discussed and condemned over glasses of stout at a long bar. Shanahan and Lamont and Furriskey do not suffer in the same way, but neither are they immune; they are bemused, they consume their lives in repetitive talk which is deliberately related to the recitals of Finn. (Compare, for instance, the leaping of Sweeney and the hag with Lamont's story of the 'jumping Irishman', Sergeant Craddock.)

O'Nolan was too much of an artist to make these points in a crude fashion. The book's impact is total. Its message is conveyed integrally, by everything that is said and done. The ironic flatness of the narrator's style, the uneventfulness of his life, are in utter contrast to the blended parody and lyricism of Finn's recitals, and also to the absurdity of the conversations between Furriskey, Shanahan, and Lamont. The three worlds are sealed off from each other, yet they go on existing side by side. And Ireland? A small, drab, orderly, modern country, haunted by an heroic past, dwarfed by an over-arching imaginative vision, its artists drinking pints of plain as the tourists walk up and down O'Connell Street and the fresh-faced country boys line up to emigrate to New York. Is there, anywhere, a better total description of Ireland than is conveyed in this book?

In case any Irishman reads this and is offended, I hasten to say that a total description of England, if one were ever achieved, would be no more flattering and certainly much less amusing. As for Wales and Scotland, they are both countries that cry out for an O'Nolan to attempt this kind of imaginative portrait. In the case of Wales, it is not difficult to blue-print the great book that might be written, if some writer with the comic talent of, say, Gwyn Thomas were also a poet who could weave material from the Mabinogion into his narrative, and make the two equally living. But the distance between Gwyn Thomas and the Mabinogion is the distance that has to be travelled; and who is to do it? In Scotland, one might perhaps say that the Lallans poets, with their insistence on assembling a vocabulary from every Scottish dialect and period, so that the language they finally arrived at was full of violent anachronisms, may have been motivated by an unformulated wish to achieve this multi-dimensional quality. But if so, all one can say is that it did not work very well. O'Nolan remains the master. He took a great deal from Joyce, as it was right and proper that he should; but he was always his own man.

I have described *At Swim-Two-Birds* at perhaps tedious length, because it seems to me, in these days when modern literature is so intensively studied, just about the only real masterpiece in English that is far too little read and discussed (the two are not always the same thing) and I was hoping to engage the interest of likely readers who have not yet sampled it. But, after all, it seems to me an impossible thing to describe. So much of it is purely atmosphere, and the atmosphere could only be conveyed by a commentary of the same length as the book. One of the things my description has entirely failed to convey is how the book's allusiveness provides it with dozens of little tap-roots to the Irish literary and social memory. Such things as the literary evening at Byrne's; the structural function of this scene is merely that Byrne, the arbiter of taste, lays down the law that everyone ought to sleep much more, thus providing a link with the two reposeful characters, the narrator and Trellis. But the mere fact that he is called Byrne, given the same name as James Joyce's closest friend in his student days at the National University, gives one's memory a tiny jog, reminding one how near at hand is this crowd of powerful ghosts. And when the narrator, wishing to annoy his uncle by staying in his room for an extra few minutes when he knows the uncle is waiting to see him, opens a book to read a page or two, the book he chooses, and from which an extract is promptly woven into the tapestry of the scene, is Falconer's *Shipwreck*, and again something stirs in us and we remember that passage from Yeats's unforgettable description of his grandfather William Pollexfen: 'He must have been ignorant, though I could not judge him in my childhood, for he had run away to sea when a boy, "gone to sea through the hawse-hole", as he put it, and I can but remember him with two books—his Bible and Falconer's *Shipwreck*, a little green-covered book that lay always on his table.'

O'Nolan's next book was *The Third Policeman*. At least, I assume it was his next, because although it was not published until 1967, the publishers then printed with the text a note by the author, dated February 1940, in which he speaks of the book as 'just finished'. This would mean that it was written within the same phase of O'Nolan's creative life as *At Swim-Two-Birds*, and it shows hardly any falling-off from the level of that masterpiece. It is, indeed, the perfect second book, showing continuity with the first while at the same time varying the idiom and breaking into new territory.

The Third Policeman resembles *At Swim-Two-Birds* in having a narrator who describes the action in a deadpan, uncoloured style; and in exploiting the comic possibilities of uneducated Irish speech; and in juxtaposing the banalities of this speech with the wildest fantasy. Beyond that, we come to the abrupt differences. The four levels of the first book are here reduced to two; the fantastic element, instead of being partly invented and partly made from a *collage* of 'old mythologies from heel to throat', is entirely invented; and the tone has altered. Where the first book was hilarious, elegiac, sarcastic, grotesque, relaxed and genial, the second is tense, grim and threatening. It describes a horrible murder in the first sentence, and in its closing pages it contains an entirely realistic picture of a man dying of fright. In between, the tension is very seldom relaxed.

To attempt anything like a synopsis of *The Third Policeman* is an even more hopeless task than to do so for *At Swim-Two-Birds*. The baroque extravagances of the author's imagination far outrun anything that could be set down in a few paragraphs. However, the shell of the book can be described quite shortly, and there will be no harm in this if the reader unacquainted with the book bears in mind that it is the shell and nothing more.

The narrator, who is not named, and about whom we know very little except that he was early left an orphan, has a wooden leg, and owns a small-holding combined with a public house, unites with a man called Divney, an ordinary country lout who works, or rather idles, on the farm and behind the bar, to kill an old miser named Mathers who lives alone and hoards money in his house. After the murder Divney refuses for three years to tell the narrator the whereabouts of the box containing Mathers's money. To forestall any attempt at a getaway, the narrator spends all his time watching Divney and even sleeps in the same bed. Finally, Divney says that the time has come to share out the contents of the box, and that, since he has kept the narrator in suspense (for good reasons of security, he insists), he will allow him to be the one who goes and gets the loot from its hiding-place. This, Divney says, is under the floor-boards in an upstairs room in Mathers's house. Divney waits at the gate while the narrator goes into the empty house and up to the room, and gropes under the floorboards. As he does so, a curious change comes over his perceptions.

I cannot hope to describe what it was but it had frightened me very much long before I had understood it even slightly. It was some change which came upon me or upon the room, indescribably subtle, yet momentous, ineffable. It was as if the daylight had changed with unnatural suddenness, as if the temperature of the evening had altered greatly in an instant or as if the air had become twice as rare or twice as dense as it had been in the winking of an eye; perhaps all of these and other things happened together for all my senses were bewildered all at once and could give me no explanation. The fingers of my right hand, thrust into the opening in the floor, had closed mechanically, found nothing at all and came up again empty. The box was gone!

I heard a cough behind me, soft and natural yet more disturbing than any sound that could ever come upon the human ear. That I did not die of fright was due, I think, to two things, the fact that my senses were already disarranged and able to interpret to me only gradually what they had perceived and also the fact that the utterance of the cough seemed to bring with it some more awful alteration in everything, just as if it had held the universe standstill for an instant, suspending the planets in their courses, halting the sun and holding in mid-air any falling thing the earth was pulling towards it. I collapsed weakly from my kneeling backwards into a limp sitting down upon the floor. Sweat broke upon my brow and my eyes remained open for a long time without a wink, glazed and almost sightless.

The cough he hears is uttered by old Mathers, his victim, who is sitting in an armchair, drinking tea and watching him. From that moment on, the story becomes entirely fantastic, but without losing its hypnotic credibility. It is dream-like, and however fantastic our dreams are, we do not disbelieve them until we wake.

What has happened, though we have to wait till the end of the book to realize it, is that Divney, wanting the narrator out of the way, has put a bomb under the floorboards and this has gone off and killed him. For the rest of the action, the man is dead, and he inhabits a drab, anxious world in which everything lies under the threat of some terrible punishment. After chatting politely with old Mathers, who seems to wish him no harm, the narrator decides to carry on with his search for the black box containing Mathers's savings, and to this end he goes to a police station. As he approaches this building, we come to one of the points in the story at which an attentive reader might suspect that the action has moved out of the world of mortality:

As I came round the bend of the road an extraordinary spectacle was presented to me. About a hundred yards away on the left-hand side was a house which astonished me. It looked as if it were painted like an advertisement on a board on the roadside and indeed very poorly painted. It looked completely false and unconvincing. It did not seem to have any depth or breadth and looked as if it would not deceive a child. That was not in itself sufficient to surprise me because I had seen pictures and notices by the roadside before. What bewildered me was the sure knowledge deeply-rooted in my mind, that this was the house I was searching for and that there were people inside it. I had no doubt at all that it was the barracks of the policemen. I had never seen with my eyes ever in my life before anything so unnatural and appalling and my gaze faltered about the thing uncomprehendingly as if at least one of the customary dimensions was missing, leaving no meaning in the remainder. The appearance of the house was the greatest surprise I had encountered since I had seen the old man in the chair and I felt afraid of it.

I kept on walking, but walked more slowly. As I approached, the house seemed to change its appearance. At first, it did nothing to reconcile itself with the shape of an ordinary house but it became uncertain in outline like a thing glimpsed under ruffled water. Then it became clear again and I saw that it began to have some back to it, some small space for rooms behind the frontage. I gathered this from the fact that I seemed to see the front and the back of the 'building' simultaneously from my position approaching what should have been the side. As there was no side that I could see I thought the house must be triangular with its apex pointing towards me but when I was only fifteen yards away I saw a small window apparently facing me and I knew from that that there must be *some* side to it. Then I found myself almost in the shadow of the structure, dry-throated and timorous from wonder and anxiety. It seemed ordinary enough at close quarters except that it was very white and still. It was momentous and frightening; the whole morning and the whole world seemed to have no purpose at all save to frame it and give it some magnitude and position so that I could find it with my simple senses and pretend to myself that I understood it. A constabulary crest above the door told me that it was a police station. I had never seen a police station like it.

The narrator enters this strange building on a trumped-up pretext of enquiring after a lost watch. Here, his sufferings begin, never to cease. The station is inhabited by two officers, Sergeant Pluck and Policeman MacCruiskeen. There is also a third policeman, Policeman Fox, who is known to operate in the vicinity and to use the station as his headquarters, but he is never seen by the other two, partly (one gathers) because he is on permanent night-duty.

The narrator is immediately caught up and involved in the strange, sinister world of Sergeant Pluck and Policeman MacCruiskeen. These two are very considerable imaginative creations; genial, slow-witted, ordinary, yet extremely sinister. Their talk is as comically banal as that of Furriskey, Lamont and Shanahan in *At Swim-Two-Birds*—who also, of course, have their sinister aspect—but their routines are a strange blend of the ordinary duties of a country constabulary, hunting for lost bicycles and so forth, and bizarre but urgent duties which involve various ways of manipulating the physical universe; as when MacCruiskeen squeezes a ray of light through a kitchen mangle in order to compress it into sound, or when the pair conduct the narrator round a horrible claustrophobic outpost of eternity where time is unknown and space is simply an infinite series of repetitions.

The two policemen know that the narrator has murdered Mathers and they courteously express their intention of hanging him; a brotherhood of one-legged men makes a gallant attempt to rescue him, but are defeated by a horrible metaphysical practical joke; then, however, the policemen are themselves the victim of an indescribable prank of this same nature and this creates a diversion which allows the narrator to escape on a stolen bicycle. Full of relief and joy, he bicycles through the deepening dusk towards his home, looking forward to resuming his normal life and seeing Divney again, but when he is almost at his own house he passes that of Mathers, and yields to the impulse to go in and search once more for the box. Various horrible things befall him during his search, but the climax of them all is that he meets a huge policeman, who has made a police station for himself within one of the thick walls of old Mathers's house. The policeman points out that the narrator has no lamp on his bicycle, and the narrator replies that it has been stolen. They go into the long, narrow police station to record the details of the theft, and there, by the lamp-light, the narrator sees to his horror that the policeman, who is of course Policeman Fox, has the face of Mathers.

Once again he nearly dies of fright, but Policeman Fox/Mathers makes no attempt to detain him and is heavily affable.

The narrator goes out, finds his bicycle and rides on to his own house. There, looking through the window, he sees Divney, fat, bald and twenty years older, with a wife and half-grown son. The narrator enters and speaks to Divney, who goes into convulsions of fright from which he never recovers; and now, with Divney going mad at the sight of him and the wife and son unable to see or hear him at all, it becomes finally obvious that he is a ghost. Divney babbles out the story of the bomb under the floor-boards and the narrator's death, and the narrator turns to walk back towards the police station. He does not know why he goes in that direction; indeed, he does not know anything:

> My feet carried my nerveless body onwards for mile upon mile of rough cheerless road. My mind was completely void. I did not recall who I was, where I was or what my business was upon earth. I was alone and desolate yet not concerned about myself at all. The eyes in my head were open but they saw nothing because my brain was void.

In this empty state, a non-being, an inhabitant of Limbo, he approaches the police station, there to find Pluck and MacCruiskeen and begin his sufferings all over again; but this time he hears footsteps hurrying after him and is joined by Divney, his fellow-murderer, who will suffer the same punishment.

As an imaginative vision of Purgatory, for such I take it to be, this story rings dreadfully true. Once again, O'Nolan had managed to make perfect use of his particular combination of gifts.

The summary I attempted above is of course entirely inadequate and in any case relates only to half the book. The sub-plot, or subordinate strand, describes the ideas of a man called de Selby, an obscure savant whose voluminous works contrive to deal, in highly eccentric fashion, with virtually every problem of civilization, metaphysics, mathematics and the physical universe. De Selby's mental world, as we glimpse it in lengthy foot-notes, is as fantastic as the world of the two policemen, than which one could hardly say more. Among his beliefs we may note the following: that night is caused not by planetary movements but by accumulations of 'black air', that human existence is 'a succession of static experiences each infinitely brief', from which it follows that motion is an illusion; that the air is composed of minute balloons and that the sharp sound of percussion is due to the bursting of 'atmosphere balls'; that the earth is sausage-shaped. The de Selby material serves two purposes. One is, of course, that of providing comic relief on a glorious scale. Not only de Selby's own rich absurdities, but the venomous controversies of his exegetes, entertain us through hilarious footnote after footnote. But there is a more serious purpose. It is when the narrator first makes the acquaintance of de Selby's work, at school, and conceives a passion for it, that his feet start on the downward path. He steals from the school library a copy of de Selby's *Golden Hours* (ironic title!) and comments explicitly, 'it was for de Selby I committed my first serious sin. It was for him,' he adds, 'that I committed my greatest sin.' For his only motive for wanting Mathers's money was to buy the leisure necessary to devote his life to the study of de Selby's thought.

The question of how far O'Nolan thought of himself as a Catholic writer is one that I cannot settle, having no biographical knowledge of him and not knowing whether he was a practising Catholic or not. But it is evident that the cast of his mind was Catholic; his work has a strong orientation towards Catholic Christianity; and perhaps I am not being fanciful in connecting the narrator's fall into mortal sin with the intellectual curiosity kindled in his immature brain by de Selby's work. After all, the Church approves of and fosters speculation only within fairly sharp limits; it has never been part of the Catholic position that intellectual hunger in itself and for its own sake is an unqualified good.

The Third Policeman was, presumably, offered for publication and rejected. I have no idea of the reasons for this, and no doubt someone will one day publish O'Nolan's *Life and Letters* and all will be made clear. Still, whatever the background, unpublished it was and unpublished it remained until 1967, after the author's death. *At Swim-Two-Birds* had made no impact on the public, largely because of the unfortunate time at which it was published, and probably *The Third Policeman* seemed to a publisher's eye to be just another eccentric and unsaleable book. The disappointment for O'Nolan must have been great. The second work is genuinely original and powerful, as good as his first book without in any way echoing it, and to have the first work neglected and the second not published at all must have been a cruel blow. He published no more novels for twenty years, a mid-career silence rivalling Milton's.

During these years, O'Nolan kept his hand in as a writer, but he chose to occupy the narrower stage of Dublin and Irish affairs generally. For twenty-six years he wrote his 'Cruiskeen Lawn' (= *Cruiscan Lan*, Flowing Jug) column of satiric extravaganza in the *Irish Times*, and this was much appreciated; a paper-back anthology of it was published in the mid-forties. His play, *Faustus Kelly*, dealing with corruption in local government, was put on by the Abbey Theatre in 1943. And at some point, I am not sure when, he wrote in Irish a satire on the Irish-language movement, *An Béal Bocht*.

Nevertheless, as a novelist, and as a contender for the attention of the large English-speaking literary public, he was silent for two decades. Then came the turning of O'Nolan's tide. In 1960 *At Swim-Two-Birds* was re-published, this time with adequate recognition. The bands played, the cheer-leaders of the literary press roared their belated approval, and the effect on O'Nolan was so galvanic that he published two novels in fairly brisk succession : *The Hard Life* (1961) and *The Dalkey Archive* (1964). Both are amusing and original; both show O'Nolan's characteristic preoccupations, and work over his familiar themes; but it must, I think, be admitted that, in those two decades, something had leaked away. The element of genius has gone; what remains is deftness and talent, the stock-in-trade of Myles na gCopaleen.

The Hard Life is sub-titled *An Exegesis of Squalor*; the word 'exegesis' has a theological undertone, and indeed the book turns out to be curiously haunted by the portly ghost of Mother Church. Two young boys, deserted by their parents, are given a home by a Dublin citizen, Mr Collopy, and his daughter, Annie. Mr Collopy is another sketch of the lower-middle-class Dubliner, like the 'uncle' of *At Swim-Two-Birds*, and the younger brother, who narrates the book, is like the nephew in being quiet, reserved, and fond of lying in bed. The elder brother, however, is a new departure into satirical farce: he is a restless projector and speculator, like a youthful Irish version of Wells's Ponderevo, launching money-making schemes one after another. The schemes turn out well for him but badly for other people; for instance, he sells a tightrope-walking set, complete with grappling irons and special boots, and a boy who buys one and tries it out is injured and almost drowned.

'The brother' soon leaves for London and continues his operations on a larger scale; the central section of the book elaborates on the relationship between Mr Collopy and a comical German Jesuit named Father Fahrt. Chapter 10, one of O'Nolan's set-pieces, consists of a long conversation between the two old cronies as they sit by the stove with a crock of whisky. This conversation, in which Mr Collopy vigorously belabours the Jesuit order and Father Fahrt mildly but firmly defends it, is not only a high spot in the book but of wide general significance for O'Nolan's work, and we shall return to it later. At the moment it is sufficient to note that the two plots run side by side. 'The brother' continues his up-to-date schemes for making money, and Mr Collopy grimly pursues an objective that has become the chief ambition of his life. What this objective is, we are never explicitly told; but it is made clear enough by various hints and references that Mr Collopy wants Dublin to be adequately supplied with women's urinals. To this end he rails against the city council, he organises a committee, and finally, in company with Father Fahrt, he goes to Rome and manages to secure an interview with the Holy Father himself. Meanwhile, Mr Collopy has been trying to alleviate his rheumatism by taking a patent medicine advertised and supplied by 'the brother'. This medicine, known as Gravid Water, has the unexpected effect of making him so enormously heavy that when climbing up some wooden steps he falls through and is killed. The book ends with the reading of

Mr Collopy's will and a brief visit from the entirely unrepentant brother. He cynically advises the narrator to consider marriage to Annie, who has been left with a house and an income. The narrator's reaction to this is to be sick, and in his 'tidal surge of vomit' the book ends.

The Dalkey Archive has the same kind of extravagant plot. But it is a wilder, more ambitious book. It does not succeed; its various parts pull away from each other and leave one with the impression of a book without a centre. Through all the farcical episodes, one has persistently the impression that O'Nolan is trying to use the story to say something that does not, finally, succeed in getting itself said. Theological overtones abound, there is an air of religious controversy and Christian symbolism over the whole book, and yet no theme, Christian or otherwise, emerges into coherence. So I felt when I first read it, and so I feel now. But the posthumous publication of *The Third Policeman* has introduced a new element into the situation; for we can now see that *The Dalkey Archive* makes use of some of the material from that lost book. Why O'Nolan decided to do this, I do not know; perhaps someone had convinced him that *The Third Policeman* was unpublishable and would never see the light; perhaps he became, for some reason, dissatisfied with it himself and wished to use some of its ideas in a book that would have a better chance of success. Whatever the reasons, he built into his new structure many of the stones from the ruins of the earlier and, it must be said, far stronger one. He introduced de Selby as a character (giving him, this time, a capital D); and he made great play with one of Sergeant Pluck's frightening philosophical theories, having to do in this case with bicycles.

Two young Dubliners—Michael Shaughnessy, the narrator, and his friend Hackett, a kind of scaled-down Buck Mulligan—are returning from a bathe in the sea at Dalkey when they meet a middle-aged man who has cut his foot and needs help to get back to his isolated house on the cliff. This man is, as the old romancers used to say, 'none other than' De Selby, no longer a shadowy presence behind a shelf of books but a mad savant who pursues the twin aims of abolishing time and at the same time obliterating life on the planet by taking all the oxygen out of the air. He has developed a substance called D.M.P. (O'Nolan's sly reference is to the initials of the Dublin Metropolitan Police) with which he intends to carry out these aims.

To avert this, Mick O'Shaughnessy arranges with Sergeant Fottrell, the local representative of the law, that the two of them shall break into De Selby's house one night and steal his supply of D.M.P. They do this, and subsequently De Selby's house is burnt down and gutted (by Hackett?) while its owner is away in London. Meanwhile, two other actions develop. Mick confides the story of De Selby to his girl-friend, Mary; a cool and sensible girl, she finds the tale incredible but nevertheless feels enough concern to make arrangements, over his head, for Mick to receive the aid of a priest in the shape of a certain Father Cobble, S.J. Mick is slightly nonplussed by this but accepts her decision and not only sees Father Cobble himself but arranges for him to talk to De Selby. The two of them visit De Selby at home, and he receives them courteously but craftily evades the subject of his plan for world destruction.

Another action now develops. From a local doctor with whom he sometimes drinks in a quiet bar at Dalkey, Mick learns that James Joyce is still alive and hiding himself in seclusion in the little watering-place of Skerries. Mick resolves to seek Joyce out, not only because of his veneration for the great Irish writer, but because it suggests a way out of the problem of dealing with De Selby. After all, he and Sergeant Fottrell can steal De Selby's supply of D.M.P., but how can De Selby be prevented from manufacturing a new supply and starting again? For 'his Christian conscience forbade the simple killing of De Selby', even to save the world.

In an interesting passage of self-examination, Mick ranges in order the problems that confront him and decides that if Joyce really is alive, and can be brought to the acquaintance of De Selby, the result might be an intellectual confusion of such gigantic proportions as to prevent either of them from doing anything at all during the remainder of their lives.

Assuming he met Joyce and won his confidence, could the contretemps . . . be resolved by bringing together De Selby and Joyce and inducing both to devote their considerable brains in consultation to some recondite, involuted and incomprehensible literary project, ending in publication of a book which would be commonly ignored and thus be no menace to universal sanity? Would Joyce take to De Selby, and vice versa? Does a man reciprocally accept a dissimilar madness?

Partly with this object in mind, and partly in the hope of pleasing Mary, who is of a literary bent, Mick wanders about Skerries and at last finds James Joyce serving behind the counter in a quiet, old-fashioned public house. Another surprise is in store. Joyce is a devout Catholic. His literary work was no more than a *jeu d'esprit*; it began and ended with *Dubliners*, written in collaboration with Oliver St John Gogarty, who at the last moment refused to allow his name to appear on the title-page because it might ruin his professional career in medicine. The encounter becomes more wildly funny as it develops:

—Very interesting. But what else have you written, mainly?

Joyce quietly attended to the ash of his cigar.

—So far as print is concerned, mostly pamphlets for the Catholic Truth Society of Ireland. I am sure you know what I mean—those little tracts that can be had from a stand inside the door of any church; on marriage, the sacrament of penance, humility, the dangers of alcohol.

Mick stared.

—You surprise me.

—Now and again, of course, I attempted something more ambitious. In 1926 I had a biographical piece on Saint Cyril, Apostle of the Slavs, published in *Studies*, the Irish Jesuit quarterly. Under an assumed name, of course.

—Yes. But *Ulysses*?

There was a low sound of impatience in the gloom.

—I don't want to talk about that exploit. I took the idea to be a sort of practical joke but didn't know enough about it to suspect it might seriously injure my name. It began with an American lady in Paris by the name of Sylvia Beach. I know it's a horrible phrase,

I detest it, but the truth is that she fell in love with me. Fancy that!

He smiled bleakly.

—She had a bookshop which I often visited in connection with a plan to translate and decontaminate great French literature so that it could be an inspiration to the Irish, besotted with Dickens, Cardinal Newman, Walter Scott and Kickham. My eye had a broad range—Pascal and Descartes, Rimbaud, de Musset, Verlaine, Balzac, even that holy Franciscan, Benedictine and medical man, Rabelais . . .!

—Interesting. But *Ulysses*?

—Curious thing about Baudelaire and Mallarmé—both were obsessed with Edgar Allan Poe.

—How did Miss Beach express her love for you?

—Ah-ha! Who is Sylvia? She swore to me that she'd make me famous. She didn't at the beginning say how, and anyhow I took it all patiently as childish talk. But her plot was to have this thing named *Ulysses* concocted, secretly circulated and have the authorship ascribed to me. Of course at first I didn't take the mad scheme seriously.

—But how did the thing progress?

—I was shown bits of it in typescript. Artificial and laborious stuff, I thought. I just couldn't take much interest in it, even as a joke by amateurs. I was immersed in those days in what was intrinsically good behind the bad in Scaliger, Voltaire, Montaigne, and even that queer man Villon. But how well-attuned they were, I thought, to the educated Irish mind. Ah yes. Of course it wasn't Sylvia Beach who showed me those extracts.

—Who was it?

—Various low, dirty-minded ruffians who had been paid to put this material together. Muckrakers, obscene poets, carnal pimps, sodomous sycophants, pedlars of the coloured lusts of fallen humanity. Please don't ask me for names.

Joyce has one ambition: to spend what remains of his life in a religious order, preferably the Society of Jesus. From this point on, the object of getting him entangled with De Selby is quietly dropped, and Mick arranges for Joyce, in his turn, to be confronted by Father Cobble. The meeting between them is the great hilarious climax of the book; having already given away enough of the plot, I will say no more, except that Mick hurries away from the scene leaving Joyce and Cobble together, comforting himself with the thought that Joyce is now in hands well qualified to take care of him. The book ends with the focus on Mary. After a long and vague relationship with Mick, she appears to be on the point of leaving him to marry Hackett; this is averted, she and Mick agree to marry, and the last words of the book are her utterly unexpected remark: 'I'm certain I'm going to have a baby.'

We can tell from these two novels, as we could not from *At Swim-Two-Birds*, that O'Nolan, whether or not he was a Catholic *croyant et pratiquant*, was deeply interested in Christian doctrine and church organisation. Both novels are loaded with Catholic lore to an extent to which my rapid summaries give no clue.

The dialogue between Mr Collopy and Father Fahrt, for instance, in Chapter 10 of *The Hard Life*, could only have been written by someone to whom the beliefs and activities of the Catholic Church were of absorbing interest. Mr Collopy gives vent to all the familiar abuse of Jesuits on the grounds of their wealth, worldliness, hypocrisy, and casuistry. It is wonderfully cathartic, and must be especially so to anyone who went through a Jesuit education. But Father Fahrt is always there to correct the wild exaggerations and put the Jesuit case.

—Oh now you can always trust a Jesuit to make mischief and complicate simple things.

—That word Jesuit. Our founder Ignatius was a Spaniard and had a different name for the Order, but it was called Societas Jesu by command of the Holy Father Paul III. Originally the title Jesuit was one of hatred and contempt. What was intended as an insult we accepted as a compliment.

—I suppose that's what I mean—you are for ever double-thinking and double-talking. You slither everywhere like quicksilver. There's no pinning a Jesuit down. Then we're told it is a mendicant order. Sure there isn't a better-got collection of men on the face of the earth, churches and palaces all over the world. I know a thing or two. I've read books. I'll tell you something about 35 Lower Leeson Street, the poor cave you hid in yourself.

—What?

—The emaciated friars in that place have red wine with their dinners. That's more than Saint Peter himself had. But Saint Peter got himself into a sort of divarsion with a cock. The holy fathers below in Clongowes Wood know all about cocks, too. They have them roasted and they eat them at dinner. And they are great men for scoffing claret.

—Such talk is most unworthy. We eat and drink according to our means. The suggestion that we are, well . . . sybarites and gluttons is nonsense. And offensive nonsense, Collopy. I do not like such talk.

—Well, is that so? Mr Collopy said testily. Is criticising the Jesuits a new sin? Would you give somebody five rosaries in the confessional for that? Faith then, if criticising the Jesuits is a fall from grace, let us say a Hail Mary for the repose of the soul of Pope Paul IV, for he told Ignatius Loyola that there were a lot of things wrong with the Order that would have to be put right. Did you know that? And did Ignatius bend the knee in front of the Holy Father? Not on your life. Give me your damn glass.

—Thanks. I do not say that Ignatius was without fault. Neither was Peter. But Ignatius was canonized in 1622 by Pope Gregory XV, only sixty-six years after his death. He is now in Paradise.

—You know he died without the last rites?

—I do. He was called suddenly. He was weak of body but his labours in this world were prodigious, and nobody can take from him credit for the great deed of founding the Order, which is now and ever has been the intellectual vanguard of the Catholic Church.

—I wouldn't say the story is quite so simple as that, Father Fahrt. By Dad, the same Order caused a lot of bad bloody ructions at one time.

—The Fathers are all over the world, they speak and write in all languages, they have built a wonderful apparatus for the propagation of the faith.

—Some people at one time thought they were trying to banjax and bewilder the One, Holy and Apostolic. Oh and there are good people who are alive today and think the Church had a very narrow escape from the boyos of yesteryear.

—I know it is useless asking who those important people are.

Father Fahrt is comical enough, and the whole scene is a joke, but it is not the kind of a joke that would occur to a non-Catholic. The same is true of the extraordinary scene in which the pair obtain an audience with the Pope, and Mr Collopy appeals to His Holiness for aid in increasing the number of conveniences for the ladies of Dublin. The Pope's startled replies are given in his own words, a mixture of Latin (when he remembers his dignity) and Italian (when he is shocked into ordinary scolding), and also in a translation supposedly provided by His Holiness's secretary, one Father Cahill. O'Nolan's outrageous dead-pan humour, a wild mixture of farce and scholarship, reaches a peak in this scene.

COLLOPY spoke.

THE POPE

Che cosa sta dicendo questo poveretto?

What is this poor child trying to say?

MONSIGNOR CAHILL spoke.

THE POPE

E tocco? Nonnunquam urbis nostrae visitendium capitibus affert vaporem. Dei praesidium hujus infantis amantissimi invocare velimus.

Is this child in his senses? Sometimes the heat of our city brings a vapour into the heads. We invoke God's protection for a beloved child.

COLLOPY spoke again.

MONSIGNOR CAHILL spoke.

THE POPE

Ho paura che abbiate fatto un errore, Eminenza, nel potar qui questo pio uomo. Mi sembra che sia un po'tocco. Forse gli manca una rotella. Ha sbagliato indirizzo? Non siamo medici che curano il corpo.

Dear Cardinal, I fear you have made a mistake in bringing this pious man to see us. I fear the Lord has laid a finger on him. We would not say that his head is working properly. Can it be that he is in the wrong place? We are not a doctor for the body.

FATHER FAHRT spoke.

THE POPE

Ma questo e semplicemente mostruoso. Neque hoc nostrum officium cum concilii urbani officio est confundendum.

But this is monstrous. Nor should our office be confused with that of a city council.

This is not, as anti-clerical satire would be, founded on the notion that the Papacy in itself is funny, that an audience with the Pope is an absurdity. On the contrary, its humour arises from the abrupt collision between the quaint fanaticism of Mr Collopy and the seriousness and dignity of the Papal presence.

If I, with my Protestant background and lack of systematic religious beliefs, find these passages funny, I should expect a Catholic to find them funnier still, unless he was entirely lacking in humour, in which case I should expect him to demand that the books should be put on the Index. In either event, the point is the same. This is Catholic writing, about Catholic matters, no less so than a full-scale attack like *A Portrait of the Artist as a Young Man* or a full-scale affirmation like the novels of G. K. Chesterton.

In *The Dalkey Archive*, as I mentioned earlier, theological argument abounds, and there are traces of an over-arching Christian symbolism. De Selby, in the earlier book the cause of the narrator's downfall into mortal sin, is here presented in the same sinister-farcical light; though, in keeping with the lighter tone of the later book, he does not succeed in doing anyone any harm. He is no unbeliever, but rather a fanatical bigot, who condemns the Church strongly for having admitted false doctrines and holds that the universal destruction of mankind is the only way to prevent God's word from becoming more and more distorted by wilful human foolishness. And James Joyce, when he appears, is very much the lifelong amateur theologian. He early reveals to Mick that a great part of his motive for wishing to become a Jesuit is to reform that order and, through it, the Church, by freeing them from the doctrine of the Trinity. To him, God is of two Persons, and the Holy Spirit was 'the invention of the more reckless of the early Fathers'. To Mick's timid remonstrance Joyce returns an unyielding scorn.

I always understood that God was of three Divine Persons.
—Well you didn't get up early enough in the morning, my lad.

The Holy Ghost was not officially invented until the Council of Constantinople in 381.

Joyce is a theologian, De Selby is a theologian; even the lout Hackett is a theologian when he has a drink inside him. Hackett's ambition, at such times, is to rehabilitate the apocryphal Gospel of Judas Iscariot. 'All the obloquy heaped on him is based on nothing but inference. I hope to have part of the Bible rewritten.' Land of saints and scholars!

The Dalkey Archive is, in fact, more thoroughly permeated with Catholicism, and Christianity generally, than *The Hard Life*. The local pub, in which the characters meet and where Mick first hears of the continued existence of James Joyce, is called the Colza Hotel, because its landlady, Mrs Laverty, '. . . was a most religious woman and once had a talk with a neighbour about the red lamp suspended in the church before the high altar. When told it was sustained with colza oil, she piously assumed that this was a holy oil used for miraculous purposes by Saint Colza, VM [Virgin Martyr], and decided to put her house under this banner.'

The other principal bit of borrowing from *The Third Policeman* is also given a more specifically theological flavour in the later book. Sergeant Pluck has a theory, which he expounds to the horrified prisoner at the police station, that when two substances are in collision a few of their molecules can change places. If a man walks along a hard road, some of the molecules of his boot-sole are driven into the road and replaced by some molecules of the road. It follows from this that anyone who rides a bicycle for some hours each day will gradually exchange molecules with his bicycle until it is somewhat human and he is somewhat velocipedal. Sergeant Pluck draws the narrator's attention to those bicycles that appear in warm, dry kitchens, not too far from the fire and within earshot of the family conversation ('Mick thinks that Pat brought it in and Pat thinks that Mick was instrumental'), and also to those human beings who show a tendency to stand with one elbow against a wall or one foot supported on the kerb.

This theory reappears in Sergeant Fottrell, and so does some of the comic by-play to which it gives rise (the policeman regularly steals a man's bicycle in order to cut down his cycling time and thus save him from this fate, etc.). But now, in the all-pervading atmosphere of theological argument, it has become more doctrinal, more reminiscent, in its wild way, of the various doctrines of transubstantiation; whereas in the earlier story it was part of the eerie, unaccountable, menacing landscape of Purgatory.

There are even hints that the colourless Mick, who is thrust suddenly into the position of having to act and perhaps sacrifice himself for the good of all humanity, is a kind of miniature Christ. The last sentence of the novel is relevant here, since Christianity itself began with Mary's saying 'I'm certain I'm going to have a baby'. Earlier on it has been specifically stated that Mary is a virgin, at any rate as far as Mick is concerned. Is she pregnant by Hackett? Or by someone unknown in the story? Or is a deeper symbolism involved?

If so, one can only say that it fails of its effect. Neither *The Hard Life* nor *The Dalkey Archive* has the authority and inclusiveness of *At Swim-Two-Birds*, nor the deep, concentrated power of *The Third Policeman.* Both the later books seem to toy with symbolic overtones rather than genuinely incorporate them. They pick their way round the edges of vitally important subjects rather than going hell-for-leather through the middle. And this realization gives us a vantage point to look back on *At Swim-Two-Birds*, noting clearly now its elegiac quality, its sense that the problems posed by time are not soluble; and also on the quietly agonized exploration of the damned state in *The Third Policeman.* If, in his first book O'Nolan came close to Joyce, in his second he anticipated the best work of Beckett. In temperament, he stands somewhere between the two. He is more discouraged than Joyce, less of a Yea-sayer. Joyce's work is bleak, but it is not elegiac. It affirms the stature of man. The eighteen hours of Leopold Bloom's life which we follow in *Ulysses* are full of shabbiness, failure, and discouragement, but they are also Homeric. Joyce's purpose in elaborating his technique of literary *son et lumière* was to affirm that his wandering Jewish salesman was no less important than Odysseus. By contrast, O'Nolan's parallels between Trellis and Sweeney, between the bardic feast and the paralytic loquacity of the saloon bar, are parallels of hopelessness. On the other hand, he is not a connoisseur of hopelessness like Beckett, who seems to have cast himself in the role of a vulture, waiting on some dusty branch for the kicking human body to become a nice quiet corpse. The sense of doom, of the curse of meaninglessness laid on all that a man is and does, is brilliantly conveyed in *The Third Policeman*, but it is set within a religious framework and shown as the punishment for taking a man's life, cruelly, for gain. In Beckett's work, the capital crime is simply to be alive; *that* is the stupidity, the evil, the appalling metaphysical *gaffe* for which we are to be snubbed and punished for ever. O'Nolan does not talk in this strain; if he lacks the gigantic affirmative energy of Joyce, he nevertheless has some of Joyce's centrality and sanity.

When, early in 1966, the news came that O'Nolan had died, I felt both saddened and amazed. Saddened that a writer who so interested and engaged me would now write no more; amazed that he was only in his early fifties. He must have been so young when *At Swim-Two-Birds* came to him; it must have formed in his mind, shaking him with laughter and dismay, at a time when he was no older than the two of us who stared down at his book, knowing that a new chapter in our own history was beginning, that morning in the Eagle and Child. *Vale.*

Dr Johnson's Poetry

As James Boswell approached the concluding pages of his *Life of Samuel Johnson, LL.D.*, he decided, lawyer-fashion, that he ought to provide a summing-up, and proceeded to gird himself for the effort of writing that 'character' of Johnson that is one of the most remarkable feats of his great book. He describes Johnson's physical appearance and presence, gives a sketch-map of his intellectual interests, outlines his moral and psychological nature and estimates the powers of his mind. In the course of these remarks, Boswell puts in two observations that are, or should be, very much in the mind of anyone approaching Johnson as a poet. One is that Johnson's mind was so fertile of imagery that 'he might have been perpetually a poet'; the other is that the imagery of Johnson's prose is more luxuriant than that of his verse.

Boswell, that is, had seen clearly two facts about Johnson which then became obscured for well over a hundred years: that he was a natural poet; and that the poetic power of his mind was, in some respects, more free to find itself in prose than in verse.

No one doubts that the ability to strike out concrete and original ideas is one of the primary features of the poetic mind. (At the present moment, with the collapse of all conventions of verse-form and a total confusion as to what constitutes 'verbal music', it is perhaps the *only* feature that is generally recognized.) All good writers have it, but the poet has it most noticeably, and carries it—as Johnson did—into his conversation as well as his formal compositions. I remember Robert Frost, talking at the table about some woman whom conventional language would have described as 'elusive' or 'mysterious'; 'She was like an orange pip on a plate,' said Frost.

If we seek to recognize Johnson's poetic quality through his imagery, the easiest way is to take any volume of his prose works and let it fall open at any point.

> Very few are involved in great Events, or have their Thread of Life entwined with the Chain of Causes on which Armies or Nations are suspended . . .

> Of the thousands and ten thousands that perished in our late contests with France and Spain, a very small part ever felt the stroke of an enemy; the rest languished in tents and ships, amidst damps and putrefaction; pale, torpid, spiritless, and helpless; gasping and groaning unpitied among men made obdurate by long continuance of hopeless misery, and whelmed in pits, or heaved into the ocean, without notice and without remembrance.

> The stream of time, which is continually washing the dissoluble fabricks of other poets, passes without injury by the adamant of *Shakespeare.*

A man who can write like this is not likely to fail completely when he attempts poetry. On the other hand, it should be admitted, most poetic conventions are limiting as well as enabling. One sees this very clearly at a time like the present, when most poets are either ranting *à la* Speakers' Corner or lisping in baby talk. But to some extent it has always been evident. Within the romantic conventions, there are some things that De Quincey's prose can do that Wordsworth's verse cannot. I think it was T. S. Eliot who laid it down, about fifty years ago, that 'Poetry should be at least as well written as prose'; but the fact is that the two forms can never achieve a regularized parity; where verse is not better than good prose, it is usually worse.

Johnson wrote poetry during most of his long life; as a schoolboy in Lichfield, he was already writing verse remarkable enough to be copied out and preserved, and one of his finest poems, the elegy on Levet, was written in the last year of his life. Not only was the making of verses a constant endeavour with Johnson, it was also a central plank in his programme of activity. Though his main concern was with wisdom ('You are a philosopher, Dr Johnson'), he never doubted that poetry was the chief human source of wisdom as well as of solace. He studied poetry, criticized it, translated it, constantly quoted and meditated on it. The most satisfying of his prose works, the *Lives of the Poets*, could only have been written by someone who had lived with English poetry for nearly seventy years, frequenting it not only as part of the essential business of his life, but also as the favourite room in his intellectual house.

With all this lifelong devotion both as reader and writer, Johnson achieved importance as a poet only in a small number of compositions. (The same could be said of Marvell, of Browning, of Dylan Thomas.) The only *indispensable* poems of Johnson are *London*, *The Vanity of Human Wishes*, the poem on Levet, and possibly the pointed and energetic *jeu d'esprit*, 'Long Expected One and Twenty'. All these poems are fairly easily available. They turn up in standard anthologies and also in such widely-disseminated one-volume selections from Johnson as Mona Wilson's in the Reynard Library (Rupert Hart-Davis) or R. W. Chapman's (Oxford University Press). So that Johnson's essential poetic achievement has long been within easy reach of anyone interested. Yet we have in recent times been presented with three complete editions of his poetry. First there was the pioneering Oxford edition by Nichol and McAdam. Then the equally elaborate edition by McAdam (the same) and Milne which appears as Volume 6 of the Yale edition of Johnson's works. Finally, Dr Fleeman's edition in the 'Penguin English Poets'. I could understand anyone who objected that, considering how small is the tip of the Johnsonian poetic iceberg, this repeated presentation of the total mass is supererogatory. Understand, but not agree.

We need all of Johnson's verse : even the admittedly unsuccessful parts of it like *Irene.* Without a sense of his solid and continuing endeavour, without that basic ground-plan of his poetic strategy which can only come from frequenting his work, we shall look uncomprehendingly even at his most shining successes. We need the feel for his language, the sound of his rhythms, sweeping all the way from the minor work to the major. We need the impromptu translations, the parodies and burlesques, for the light they shed on Johnson's approach to the poetic art. (For instance, Johnson made two translations of a passage from the *Medea* of Euripides; one in mockery of the tumid style of Robert Potter's then celebrated version, the other serious; to compare the two is to see at once what Johnson thought poetic language should, and should not, be called upon to do; it sheds light not only on Johnson's own practice, but on the reasons for his detestation of, say, Gray's Odes.) We need the theatrical prologues and epilogues for their testimony that, failure though Johnson was as a dramatic poet, he knew well how to write verse to be declaimed from a stage—that is, his deficiency as a dramatic poet is imaginative and not stylistic.

And, of course, with Johnson as with any poet, we need a sense of the literary culture within which his work roots itself: what poets were current, which of the abiding classics were at that time read as living writers are read, what knowledge could be assumed in the reader. All Johnson's work is founded in a civilization that rates literature very high and knows it well. The rich, complex allusiveness of the Juvenalian satires is not, essentially, disqualified or discounted by the bare directness of the elegy on Levet; for even in that stark, unadorned, bitterly honest poem, one feels the pressure of a set of social assumptions, the whisper that a man devoid of polite learning is not a fit subject for an elegiac poem:

> Nor, letter'd arrogance, deny
> Thy praise to merit unrefin'd.

In his own day, Johnson's reputation as a poet was founded on the two satires adapted from Juvenal; *London* (Juvenal's Third) and *The Vanity of Human Wishes* (Juvenal's Tenth). *London* established his reputation, and *The Vanity of Human Wishes* buttressed and solidified it. We can hardly do better than approach his poetry by this same avenue, if only because eighteenth-century poetry (till mid-century, at least) was in general highly allusive and the use of continuous allusion in these two poems will give us a perception of Johnson's solidarity with his culture.

Allusion has many uses. Its application may be casual and glancing, or sustained and purposive. The most important thing to grasp, however, is that allusion is part of the texture of a poem rather than its paraphrasable content. Allusion does not state: it enacts. It is a feature of the physical bearing of the poem, the way it carries itself. What, for example, is Joyce's *Ulysses* conveying by means of its continuous parallel with the *Odyssey*? What is that large-scale allusion 'saying'? (And I hope no one will bring up the irrelevant objection that *Ulysses* is 'not a poem'. It is more a poem than most verse compositions.) The back-projection from Homer, behind Mr Bloom's day in Dublin, is *enacting* a whole series of judgments rather than stating them.

Johnson, at the time of writing *London*, was a hungry fighter. Recently arrived in the metropolis after a depressing series of failures in the Midlands, living very close to the possibility of a failure so total that it would involve destitution, he was in a hurry to make his name. That he should choose to do so by means of 'imitation' was a mark of his willingness to play for big stakes, since Pope's brilliant series of 'Imitations of Horace' was very much the reigning toast in poetry, and one of the best of them came out in that same year of 1738. Johnson also chose a point of departure that would force the reader to judge his work by the highest standards. Both Dryden and the younger poet whom Dryden so generously admired, John Oldham, had worked over Juvenal's Third Satire.

Johnson's cool choice of difficult ground to fight over would convey a great deal to the eighteenth-century connoisseur, the 'wit' whose approbation could make the new reputation, before a line of his poem had been read. But there were many other choices. The whole technique of allusion, in fact, presents the writer with a continuous series of choices. Johnson could count on a readership who knew Juvenal's poem about as well as a bookish person of our time knows, say, *Vanity Fair.* When he departed from Juvenal, he would have to depart in a definite direction and the reader would spot that direction. From line to line, the poem would involve the reader in a strenuous game, an exercise in quick-wittedness.

As an old man, Johnson looked back on this kind of writing with a certain disapproval. 'Such imitations', he wrote in his *Life of Pope*, 'cannot give pleasure to common readers. The man of learning may be sometimes surprised and delighted by an unexpected parallel; but the comparison requires knowledge of the original, which will likewise often detect strained applications. Between Roman images and English manners there will be an irreconcilable dissimilitude, and the work will be generally uncouth and party-coloured; neither original nor translated, neither ancient nor modern.'

This is the wisdom of age. But it was the *young* Johnson who wrote *London*, and young poets are generally more interested in displaying their brilliance than in 'giving pleasure to common readers'. And the Johnson of the 1780s did at least put his finger on the kind of success that the Johnson of the 1730s was aiming at. 'The man of learning may be sometimes surprised and delighted by an unexpected parallel'—and if it is a little 'strained', who cares? It is like the difference between the Eliot of the *Waste Land* and the Eliot of the *Four Quartets*; wisdom has come in at one door, and pyrotechnics and brilliant showing-off have gone out through the other. And there is something in us that regrets the loss as it welcomes the gain.

To erect a modern poem on the scaffolding of an ancient one is also an affirmation. It testifies to a faith in the enduring truth of literature. If what Juvenal said about Rome is still true, *mutatis mutandis*, about eighteenth-century London, that serves as a demonstration of the strength and durability of Juvenal's satire. By implication, it also justifies the faith that the new satire, too, may live on under another sky. And this still holds good if the allusion is used ironically, if there is a deliberately exploited gap between the loftiness of the allusion and the lowness of the context in which it appears. When Eliot, in *The Waste Land*, says of the crowd flowing over London Bridge

I had not known death had undone so many,

he is quoting a line near the beginning of Dante's *Inferno*, not merely to strengthen his poem with a telling allusion ('These people remind me of the damned in Dante's vision of hell'), but also to affirm his belief in the strength of Dante's vision ('Damnation is damnation wherever you find it; my experience, for what it is worth, confirms his.') Juvenal was given to quoting fragments of Homeric epic verse amid his denunciations of modern decadence, so that the juxtaposition would make the modern look even more sordid; Johnson uses this allusive poet as the basis of his own continuous allusion; he sees European literature as a self-perpetuating and self-bracing structure, and this underwrites the solid confidence in the value of a writer's life that comes out in all his judgments. 'The chief glory of every people arises from its authors', he writes in the Preface to the Dictionary, seventeen years after *London*, and he *means* it.

Altogether, and taking account of the historical circumstances, one cannot avoid feeling that the later Johnson was being unnecessarily severe on the earlier. To say, in the eighteenth century, that 'such imitations cannot give pleasure to common readers', one must have in mind a very common reader indeed. A knowledge of Latin was then very general among educated people; it is noteworthy that, though Johnson seldom wrote any formal criticism of Latin poetry, he shows, casually, an intimate knowledge not only of classical but neo-Latin literature. More, he takes it for granted that some, at least, of his readers will share this knowledge and interest. The *Lives of the Poets* is peppered with references to modern Latin poetry. Comparing Milton's early Latin verse with its predecessors in England, he says, 'If we produced anything worthy of notice before the elegies of Milton, it was perhaps Alabaster's *Roxana*.' And in the *Life of John Philips*, commenting on a Latin ode by that poet, he says casually, 'It seems better turned than the odes of Hannes'. In the *Life of Rochester* he even transcribes, in full, a two-page Latin poem by one Passerat, merely because it is interesting and 'not common'. Obviously he has in mind the lettered country gentleman who does not find it convenient to travel and consult libraries, and likes to share in a good thing. (People like his father's customers in the country houses of Staffordshire in the early decades of the century.)

If the elderly Johnson can cater so liberally for a classical taste, it seems hard to imply blame for the younger Johnson's desire to 'surprise and delight' the reader who is a good Latinist. When *London* was published, Johnson insisted on having the more immediate relevant passages from Juvenal printed at the foot of the page, so that the reader, without the trouble of looking up, could see the neater strokes of the adaptation. It is true that the result is 'party-coloured' and 'neither original nor translated', but so are many much admired poems, e.g. Ezra Pound's *chinoiseries* or Robert Lowell's *Imitations.* When, in later years, Johnson poured contemptuous scorn on Macpherson's Ossian as a 'translation' of a non-existent original, he might have reflected that Macpherson, in his turn, was producing an 'imitation', adapting to eighteenth-century taste a pattern handed down from antiquity; the difference being that in the case of 'Ossian' the inherited pattern was not an actual, consultable work but a large general idea, the idea of primitive and romantic grandeur.

So much by way of excusing Johnson's exhibited cleverness in *London.* In larger outline, the shift from Juvenal to Johnson is obvious enough. Johnson is less scurrilous; he tones down the virulence, the pelting scabrous detail, of Juvenal's tirade; he is not, in that sense, a natural satirist. His speciality is the acute diagnosis of error and weakness, and the solemn warning; he takes no pride in his power to scold. When Juvenal beats down, Johnson strives to lift. The tone of his poem is sombre and accusatory, but the passion that flows through its positives, those areas where it finds something to praise and recommend, is, if anything, stronger than the feeling of revulsion.

One sees this clearly in the scene-setting. Johnson follows Juvenal in the narrative framework of the poem. In both, a stern and dignified patriot is shaking the dust of the city off his feet—'Umbricius' in Juvenal, 'Thales' in Johnson. He halts at the exit of the city to make a farewell oration, which is listened to submissively by the poet, the 'I' of the poem; finally, with the prophecy that one day the poet, too, will find the city finally intolerable, he stalks off. Now, Juvenal has Umbricius halt at the gate on the Appian Way; a place hallowed by patriotic associations, but now disfigured by the sordid dwellings of squatting foreigners, etc., etc. Johnson, aiming at a more positive note, has Thales take a boat from Greenwich, birthplace of Elizabeth I, and he and his companion allow a deliberate pause while their hearts overflow with patriotic emotion.

> On *Thames's* Banks, in silent Thought we stood,
> Where Greenwich smiles upon the silver Flood;
> Struck with the Seat that gave Eliza birth,
> We kneel, and kiss the consecrated Earth;
> In pleasing Dreams the blissful Age renew,
> And call Britannia's Glories back to view;
> Behold her Cross triumphant on the Main,
> The Guard of Commerce, and the Dread of *Spain.*

Johnson is, of course, being pointedly topical here, since Elizabeth had been the scourge of Spain, a nation with whom the English were currently having trouble and against whom they were in fact about to fight the 'War of Jenkins's Ear'. He is also, more discreetly, reflecting a personal alignment; he was lodging at Greenwich when he wrote the poem, and the constant sight of Inigo Jones's masterpiece must have recalled to his mind a more exalted dynasty on the English throne. The reference to Greenwich thus takes its place beside the loving mention of 'Trent' as a river typifying pastoral calm and the rural virtues. And here we abut on to the question of the poem's personal, even autobiographical qualities.

One of the most attractive and compelling features of all Johnson's writings is its very individual blend of the personal with the highly universalized. His tone is magisterial, his language presses always towards generalization, and yet Johnson, the man himself, is always palpably present. He never hesitates to make a personal utterance, even in contexts which would seem to demand an entirely neutral, impersonal note. The *locus classicus* here is, of course, the Preface to the Dictionary, with its moving self-portrait, concretely presenting a certain man in a certain situation.

> In the hope of giving longevity to that which its own nature forbids to be immortal, I have devoted this book, the labour of years, to the honour of my country, that we may no longer yield the palm of philology, without a contest, to the nations of the continent. The chief glory of every people arises from its authors: whether I shall add any thing by my own writings to the reputation of *English* literature, must be left to time: much of my life has been lost under the pressure of disease; much has been trifled away; and much has always been spent in provision for the day that was passing over me . . .

Re-reading such a passage, one thinks also of the personal fragments embedded in the *Lives of the Poets*—tributes to dead friends, scraps of reminiscence—as well as the constant pressure of Johnson's own stated beliefs and prejudices, like a steadily running tide, against which everything has to make its way; and the personal and autobiographical snatches in the *Dictionary* (*Salve, magna parens* after the mention of Lichfield, etc.); and of such vignettes from life as Johnson hastily composing the great *Rambler* on Procrastination while the printer's boy stood by for the copy and carried it off sheet by sheet, because Johnson had procrastinated.

Johnson was a great writer. But he was not every kind of great writer. In some of the qualities for which one goes to major literature, he was notably deficient. He had none of that soaring imagination which can leave the individual consciousness and site itself, for the time being, in a consciousness altogether different. When Goldsmith said that Johnson could never have written an Aesopian fable about little fishes because he would have made them all talk like whales, he meant that he would have made them talk like Johnson. Everybody in Johnson's works talks like Johnson: not necessarily in idiom—in some of the *Rambler* essays he shows quite a deft hand at realistic dialogue—but inasmuch as they utter Johnsonian moral perceptions.

I believe that Johnson was a great autobiographer. His life continually and directly fed his work. When he writes movingly and memorably, which is very often, he does so because he is passing on to us some lesson he has learnt in the intense and unremitting struggle of his life. He is not, strictly speaking, an imaginative writer. He has the moral imagination, but he lacks the kind of imagination that underlies fiction and the drama. Hence the curious demand for literal truthfulness that is such a limiting factor in his criticism. And the failure of *Irene*, which we will come to in a moment. And the under-valuing of contemporary masterpieces such as *Gulliver's Travels* and *Tristram Shandy*.

This lack is a limitation in Johnson. But there is a compensating strength. Because his mind does not travel over the whole range represented by literary creation at its broadest, it concentrates like an enormous burning-glass at the point where it operates. His way of growing was to meditate intensely on his own experience and the experience which life brought under his immediate view. Then, when he came to write, he passed this personal truth through the distilling apparatus of his style, and it emerged as—almost—universal. Almost. There is still a flavour of Johnson about it. We feel, as we read, the urgency and directness of a personal statement, a handing-on of costly experience.

If it were not for the stylistic transmutation, the continual tension between Johnson's personal way of seeing things and his generalized way of saying them, we might be left with a body of work capable of enjoying a considerable vogue at this moment. At present, the whole imaginative side of literature, the ability to take root in an alien consciousness and interpret it from within, is neglected. The catch-cries are all in favour of the confessional, the directly self-revelatory. The highest praise goes to the writer who most energetically documents the ultimate, sickening recesses of his personal doubts and weaknesses and failures. It is no accident that the trendiest books of our day are either masturbatory fantasies, like Henry Miller's *Sexus*, or are actually concerned with masturbation. If they are not, they are usually the ravings of a drug-addict. Tell me the truth—but only if it is alienated enough! In this atmosphere, Johnson's work becomes invisible because of its grave, classical, generalized language and its avoidance of detail. He writes as befits a man who can say, 'Nothing can please many, and please long, but just representations of general nature'. And to represent 'general nature' is not to avoid detail but to process it, to gather up a mass of it and squeeze out the essence.

Thus, where a Balzac or a Turgenev gives us the essential quality of his experience in the form of fable, or a Keats or a Valéry in the form of free-standing metaphor, Johnson specializes in the direct address. Behind his most generalized homily we see him, plainly, standing there. It is not merely truth he is offering us, it is Johnson's truth. It comes to us strained through the fibres of his individual being.

With this in mind, let us turn again to his poetry. And first, back to *London*, for we have not yet finished with that remarkable poem.

Some readers, their minds full of the image of Johnson the great Londoner, have found an amusing discrepancy between the sentiments expressed in *London*—the revulsion from the city, the longing for rural quiet and self-possession—and the opinions they associate with Johnson the man ('the full tide of human existence is at Charing Cross', etc., etc.). In their eyes, this discrepancy has reduced the poem to the status of a 'literary exercise' (a phrase, in itself, full of pitfalls for the superficial thinker). But if biographical canons are to be applied at all, they surely work the other way. When Johnson wrote *London*, he had been in the metropolis hardly more than a year; moreover, he was not—very much not—the kind of provincial who does not feel that he is living until he achieves the status of a Londoner. He had tried very hard, for many years, to establish himself in the Midlands, and even after going to London and throwing in his lot with Grub Street he still nourished the ideal of a quiet life in the country, for he soon returned to Staffordshire on a visit lasting many months, during which he renewed his efforts to find a schoolmastering post. Only after renewed, and final, discouragement did he return to the city.

London, to the mature Johnson, was a territory full of dangers and opportunities which he had conquered and within which his authority was unchallenged. (When George III, tipped off at his own request that Dr Johnson was in the Library, went there to seek converse with him, it is evident that there was some doubt, in the minds of both men, as to who was granting audience to whom.) To the young Johnson, a newcomer without money or influential friends, and knowing himself conspicuously deficient in the 'arts of pleasing', London must have seemed terrifyingly noisy, violent, dirty and cruel, while at the same time resplendent with prizes to be won. After the quiet streets and squares of Lichfield, it must have seemed a roaring arena; after the close-knit society he was used to, the overlapping circles of trade, cathedral and garrison, it must have seemed freezingly impersonal and indifferent.

If London repelled and scared Johnson, it must also, at other times, have put him on his mettle. Most young men, especially if they are potential artists, spend much of their formative years in a pendulum-swing between fierce exultation in the consciousness of their power, and depressed misgivings which occasionally intensify into panic. *London* is moving and memorable because it expresses both these states of mind at once. The strong, emphatic rhythms, the densely-packed language, and the continuous display of literary virtuosity, come from the exultation of a young mind conscious of its strength: the revulsion, the very genuine recoil from the chaos and cruelty of the big city, come from the distress of the same mind forced into a situation of loneliness in an environment it cannot control.

The Vanity of Human Wishes, Johnson's other fabric stretched over the framework of Juvenal, is a calmer performance, more stately and generalized. In printing it, he dispensed with the apparatus from Juvenal; the manipulation of a parallel was no longer so important. Having shown what he could do in that direction, he chose this time a poem in which Juvenal himself is more dignified and general, less scurrilous and scolding. In this poem, too, Johnson is more nearly the equal of Juvenal, whose strength as a poet (as far as I can judge) appears to lie in the gloomy epigrammatic power of his language; he is full of terse, loaded phrases (*anem et circenses*, for instance, or *quis custodiet ipsos custodes?*) which have gone on being quoted, down the centuries, by people who do not know whom they are quoting. What Johnson loses in the excitement and immediacy of *London* he gains in a settled strength of language, a steady thrust that is like the thrust of Dryden but more stately and less bounding. It is a poem that speaks particularly to those with a taste for the classical, the anti-idiosyncratic; T. S. Eliot particularly admired the set-piece *exemplum* of Charles X of Sweden (lines 191–222), and one can see why; it is a generalized portrait, a 'character', like *Gerontion.*

The power of Johnson's poetic language, as put forth in *The Vanity of Human Wishes* and the poems that belong with it, has not, in recent years, gone unrecognized. There is, notably, that fine essay by F. R. Leavis in *The Common Pursuit*, where he comes very close to a sufficient critical definition of what Johnson is doing :

> the style is remarkable for body. It is a generalizing style; its extraordinary weight is a generalizing weight . . . Johnson's abstractions and generalities are not mere empty explicitnesses substituting for the concrete; they focus a wide range of profoundly representative experience—experience felt by the reader as movingly present.

The last phrase, about the 'movingly present' experience behind Johnson's general statements, seems to be Dr Leavis's way of expressing that same sense of Johnson as a great autobiographer, a writer who constantly brings his own experience before the seat of direct judgment, which I was struggling to express earlier in this essay. And we can, with equal profit, follow up his hint about the 'generalizing weight' of Johnson's style. It is a style that manages to blend a high degree of concreteness and visuality with a correspondingly high level of generality.

The thrust is always towards some statement that will be true in a large majority of cases. ('Nothing will please many, and please long, but just representations of general nature.') We can see this powerful blend in action in any representative passage: the lines on Wolsey, for example.

In full-blown Dignity, see *Wolsey* stand,
Law in his Voice, and Fortune in his Hand:
To him the Church, the Realm, their Pow'rs consign,
Thro' him the Rays of regal Bounty shine,
Turn'd by his Nod the Stream of Honour flows,
His Smile alone Security bestows:
Still to new Heights his restless Wishes tow'r,
Claim leads to Claim, and Pow'r advances Pow'r;
Till Conquest unresisted ceas'd to please,
And Rights submitted, left him none to seize.
At length his Sov'reign frowns—the Train of State
Mark the keen Glance, and watch the Sign to hate.
Where-e'er he turns he meets a Stranger's Eye,
His Suppliants scorn him, and his Followers fly;
At once is lost the Pride of aweful State,
The golden Canopy, the glitt'ring Plate,
The regal Palace, the luxurious Board,
The liv'ried Army, and the Menial Lord,
With Age, with Cares, with Maladies oppress'd,
He seeks the Refuge of Monastic Rest.
Grief aids Disease, remember'd Folly stings,
And his last Sighs reproach the Faith of Kings.

Concise, weighty, strongly rhythmical, the lines make everything work and set everything in motion. There is no tendency here to stand back from the subject and pass it inertly in review. This is obvious enough in those three lines whose verbs all turn on facial and ocular expressions—

At length his Sov'reign frowns—the Train of State
Mark the keen Glance, and watch the Sign to hate.
Where-e'er he turns to meet a Stranger's Eye . . .

—but the mixture is even better in those passages where Johnson is frankly dealing with abstractions, but abstractions at work, demonstrating their power:

> Still to new Heights his restless Wishes tow'r,
> Claim leads to Claim, and Pow'r advances Pow'r.

The most characteristic line of all, perhaps, is

> Turn'd by his Nod the Stream of Honour flows.

Here, the image is intensely concrete. The statesman's nod is like the flick of a powerful switch that instantly diverts in its source some colossal force like electric current. We *see* the 'stream of honour' turning in its course in response to the slight and casual physical movement—a 'nod'—and the image is powerful and actual. On the other hand, the actualities of 'honour'—this or that lucrative appointment, this or that outward mark of respect and social standing—remain unparticularized.

It is this quality in Johnson's language that makes all talk of 'personification' so thin and meaningless. When we read eighteenth-century poetry in a hurry or with fatigued attention, we register the fairly frequent occurrence of nouns which have a general signification and which usually sport a capital letter. This we call Personification, and the category passes into the text-books. Eighteenth-century poets used Personification: it expressed their stately, generalized view of life; they saw experience in terms of a classical frieze, of 'storied urn and animated bust', and their language reflected it. But as soon as we begin to lean on this notion of Personification, it gives way like all words which try to define linguistic effects. ('Onomatopoeia', for instance.) When a poet like Johnson uses a noun, he nearly always pushes it some of the way towards general, emblematic applicability. If he pushes it all the way, we can fairly call the result Personification, and if we are busily engaged in modernizing his text we can signal this by a capital letter. ('Fame and Victory can hover over a standard', etc.) But as soon as we have made this decision, we are committed to a policy which uses capitalization in a limiting way, negatively as well as positively; if we *don't* capitalize the initial letter, it isn't personification, if we do, it is. This makes the Augustan use of language seem much more rigid and schematic than in fact it is. Johnson, to come back to him, uses a full degree of personification rather rarely, but a lesser degree habitually. In the last couplet of the passage quoted above, 'Grief', 'Disease' and 'Folly' are all very nearly allegorized and personified, but not quite; and when he goes definitely over the border and uses a full personification, as in l. 215, 'But did not Chance at length her Error mend?' the effect is not different enough to justify an isolating badge like capitalization. That, in brief, is the case against modernizing Johnson's text, as the Yale and Oxford editions do and as the Penguin does not. The Yale edition remarks, a trifle smugly, that it 'reduces capitalization and italics to modern usage'. But there is no 'modern usage' that corresponds to the kind of poetic language Johnson is using. Modern writers simply don't use language with that degree of generality; if they did, they would be postulating a social infrastructure that is just not there.

The instinctive naturalness with which Johnson uses this kind of language—concrete and abstract at the same time—is illustrated by the fact that he dosn't seem to have heard of the rule that Personification has to have a capital letter and Non-Personification must do without one. He scatters capitals everywhere in *London* and *Vanity*; on the other hand, in the elegy on Levet, certain words whose force is obviously so general as to amount to personification are given without capitals:

> In misery's darkest caverns known,
>   His useful care was ever nigh,
> Where hopeless anguish pour'd his groan,
>   And lonely want retir'd to die.

The generalizing weight of Johnson's language has another function. It acts as a necessary counterpoise to the crushing bulk of his personality. It keeps his utterance at a distance from the self, while allowing the self to be adequately defined within it. This kind of distancing is essential to all Johnson's imaginative work, all that work in which he offers the reader a story or a poem rather than a piece of direct instruction or admonition. It is, in fact, one of the ways in which his work as an artist separates itself from his work as a moralist. The two are, as we have seen, so close as to be in some respects indistinguishable. Johnson must have felt, whether consciously or not, that his work in poetry and fiction needed to be marked off in some decisive way from those utterances in which he was magisterial and counselling. Accordingly, we see him seeking always for some framework of dramatization and distancing. In the Juvenal satires he had the *persona* of the ancient poet and the parallel between Rome and England. In that large proportion of his work which is in one degree or another satiric, we have the insistent presence of the play-element, the strong flavour of burlesque or parody which concentrates attention on the manner of saying rather than the matter conveyed, and this again moves us away from the purely personal centre and shades the intense glare of Johnson's naked personality. There is a third means to which he often resorted: the fabulous setting, the deliberate transposition of the action into an unreal (usually an oriental) landscape.

It is here that we approach *Irene*. This crucial and revealing failure cannot be estimated apart from all that category of Johnson's work that we might call the oriental-fantastic. This would take in *Rasselas* and also such shorter things as 'The Three Fountains' and also, though for once it is not oriental, 'The Hermit of Teneriffe'. The roots of all the work in this category are three-fold.

First, there is the normal eighteenth-century machinery of the 'oriental tale'. In the effort to bring to bear a satiric focus on society—and that great age of self-consciousness provided a continuous satiric commentary on its own proceedings—the necessary initial step was to find a leverage *outside* the society. The polite, ironic, unfathomable oriental was obviously an attractive choice here. A pair of shrewd, slanting eyes behind which one could postulate an ancient civilization, without too much hampering knowledge of what that civilization actually entailed, made the perfect peep-holes for the satirist. Hence the proliferation of such works as Montesquieu's *Lettres Persanes.* From this point of view, Johnson can be seen as playing his own individual game within a well-understood set of rules.

But there was more. Johnson was a lifelong student of manners, customs, civilizations. The description of a poet's lifework in *Rasselas* (Chapter 11) is doubtless to some extent ironic, but there is no irony in the prescription that the poet 'trace the changes of the human mind as they are modified by the various institutions and accidental influences of climate or custom'. He would, it is certain, have welcomed the opportunity to roam the earth and see these climates and customs for himself. The old caricature of Johnson, largely derived from Macaulay, as an inveterate Londoner who had no standard of comparison except with what went on 'within the bills of mortality', is simply a misconception. If Johnson spent twenty years in London without travelling anywhere, that is because he was too poor to afford it. From the time he got his pension he made an extended trip every summer; he went with the Thrales to France and was disappointed when they cancelled a subsequent trip to Italy on which he was to have gone along; he visited North Wales and Brighton; he took an arduous jaunt round the Hebrides in his sixties. Further, all his life he devoured the literature of travel, and made an important contribution to it in his *Journey to the Western Islands.* But he ended that book with a reminder to the reader that the thoughts he has been sharing are the thoughts of 'one who had seen but little'. He knew that his life had been deficient in opportunities for first-hand observation. He knew that others knew far more than he did about the infinite variation of human customs and beliefs, and whenever possible he urged them to put their knowledge on record.

These two roots entwine with a third. Johnson's reading of travel-literature shaded into his lifelong fondness for romances. It was a taste he was rather ashamed of; in his criticism he is careful to draw a distinction between the kind of writing that ministers to truth and the kind that is merely fanciful. Being himself indolent and an easy prey to slothful reverie—often, it is clear, of a kind that seriously distressed the moralist in him—he felt in duty bound not to encourage the potentially bad habit of day-dreaming. But his taste for romance, for the free-floating story of marvels in a exotic setting, persisted. It took hold of him during those long days of browsing among the stock in his father's shop and it never left him. Naturally the frontier between serious study and romance-devouring was a shadowy one. His first extended work was a translation from the Latin of Father Lobo's *Voyage to Abyssinia*, a serious work by a Jesuit missionary. But if Abyssinia was an object of strict scientific survey, it remained also a place of the mind. The Abyssinia of which Rasselas is Crown Prince is not the Abyssinia of Lobo.

The oriental-fantastic side of Johnson's work comes out of this mixed soil. First, it is standard eighteenth-century procedure. Then, it ties in with Johnson's curiosity about men and manners. Third, it is an attempt to grow some useful crops on that marshy ground within himself which he feared and distrusted.

Within this framework, we can see readily enough that *Rasselas* and the shorter fables are successful, while *Irene* is a failure. The reason lies in the greater physical concreteness of the drama. Contrary to Johnson's expressed belief, a 'dramatick exhibition' is not 'a book, recited with concomitants that increase or diminish the effect'. Or, if we accept this definition, it must be with the recognition that the 'concomitants' can add or take away so much that they become more important than the book. In a prose fiction like *Rasselas*, we can placidly accept that the Afro-oriental setting is a dado. But *Irene* is meant to be acted by living men and women. As a story of love, jealousy and sacrifice, it has to be warm and breathing. The eastern setting has either to be made actual or convincing, or laid aside. In effect, Johnson does neither. His effort to splice together the day-dreaming side of his mind with the realistically-perceiving side leaves him with the two halves in his hands. And the spectacle brings suddenly to mind his own dismissive comment on Milton's highly elaborated but deeply passionate *Lycidas*: 'Where there is leisure for fiction there is little grief.' Johnson seems there to be saying that 'fiction', including both purely imaginative representation and the deployment of copious illustration from myth and legend, is incompatible with the expression of deep personal emotion: an opinion disproved over and over again in the literature of the world. To Johnson, 'fiction' seems to indicate the kind of trifling that is the product of 'leisure', rather than the imaginative lava that forces itself up through the rocks of experience. His *leisure* is not at all the same thing as Wordsworth's *tranquillity.* And while the judgment is totally untrue of *Lycidas*, it is, regrettably, true of *Irene*, which remains a poem for voices. A radio production of it would be interesting.

In *Irene*, the balance between Johnson's need to speak directly to his audience and his need for a controlling *persona* is lost. It is more successfully maintained in the Latin poetry. One of the most useful features of Dr Fleeman's edition is that it gives us literal prose translations, from the pen of Professor J. P. Sullivan, of all Johnson's Latin poems. These are, we see at once, far more intimate and confessional than his English poems. In fact, the poem he wrote on completion of the Dictionary is, outside his *Prayers and Meditations*, the most direct expression we have of his personal unhappiness, his anxiety and sense of frustration.

Irene and *The Vanity of Human Wishes* appeared in the same year, the one on the boards, the other in print. Johnson must have been consoled for the failure of the one by the solid success of the other. Many people found, or affected to find, *Vanity* a densely obscure poem; but its solidity strongly reinforced Johnson's reputation. In the next ten years, this reputation was raised higher and higher. But the works that raised it were in prose, and they were scholarly and meditative. The *Rambler* essays; the Dictionary; *Rasselas*; a host of minor works all keeping to the same high standard; it was a wonderful decade. During it, Johnson blossomed as a prose-writer the equal of Gibbon or Burke. His reputation as a poet stood still. The verse he wrote during this and the next decade was largely occasional and fleeting; much of it, being concerned with parody, belongs essentially with his criticism. During this whole stretch, there is nothing in verse that equals in sonority, in passion, in grave and stately impressiveness, the great prose utterances; the *Rambler* on capital punishment, the Preface to the Dictionary, the review of Soame Jenyns, the letter to the King on behalf of Dr Dodd. In such writing, Johnson moves with the strength of a giant, at his own pace and in his own rhythm. To such harmonies, there is nothing that the prescribed forms of eighteenth-century verse can add. To such weight, there is no extra force that the compression of the couplet or the finality of rhyme can bring. Johnson has outgrown his poetic overcoat.

And there, we might have had to leave it—if Robert Levet had not died before his friend and employer. Levet, the gruff old quack doctor who acted as M.O. to Johnson's strange and peevish household; Levet, who surely knew more of the secrets of Johnson's melancholia and fear of madness than anyone else, but who carried the knowledge to his grave. A year or two previously, writing his *Life of Gray*, Johnson had given some indication (we can see now, looking backward) that he himself had not quite reaped his full harvest as a writer. Gray was obviously a type who annoyed Johnson; fastidious, retired, living in comfort, keeping his distance from the sweat and filth of ordinary existence; his poems seemed to Johnson academic in the bad sense—literary and far-fetched. But Gray had written the *Elegy*—the great eighteenth-century poem on the death of ordinary people. The sudden explosion of praise with which Johnson greets the *Elegy*, when he arrives at it, may reflect an uneasy sense that he has been too hard on Gray, a relief at finding something he can unequivocally praise; but I feel, too, that there is a certain pain at the root of its vehemence; Johnson is determinedly praising a man he doesn't like, because that man has done a job that he, Johnson, really ought to have done. It was Johnson, who had known toil and hunger, Johnson, who had beaten the pavement all night without the price of a bed, Johnson, who came from the people and identified with them, who ought to have written the great celebration of the dead villagers, 'their useful toil, Their humble joys and destiny obscure'. And this ironic, fastidious don had done it!

Johnson's praise of Gray's *Elegy* is a generous handing-over of laurels that ought to have been his. But the story was not over. The *Life of Gray* was written some time about 1780. Levet died in January 1782, Johnson himself in December 1784. The elegy on Levet is the only considerable work of these two last miserable years; in some ways it is the crowning work of Johnson's life. It universalizes the particular experience without one invented detail or one conventional sentiment. It is a nugget of pure truth.

Boswell records that Johnson recited the verses to him, on 21 March 1783, 'with an emotion which gave them full effect'. Anyone who cares for Johnson's poetry would give a great deal, I think, to go back in time and eavesdrop on that recital. In the elegy on Levet, we hear, perhaps for the only time in his verse, the voice of Johnson speaking with entire directness: no *persona*, no ventriloquial substitutions, no element of parody or implied critique of a mode of expression. This is not invariably a recipe for the best poetry; some poets, when they speak directly from their experience, reveal nothing but the thinness of that experience and the self-regarding manner in which they have reacted to it; they are more interesting when they can erect a literary structure. But it is the particular nature of Johnson's case that the strength of his work comes, very directly, from the strength of his character. Levet, coarse and morose and unqualified as he was, stood Johnson in good stead not only as a 'social comfort' but as—what his nature demanded—a moral example. He was the steward with the single talent who had not allowed it to lie idle. Commonplace as his gifts were, he had rendered a good account of them. So that the sudden and merciful ending of his long life, coming at a time when Johnson was preparing for his own death, released a deep spring of feeling in Johnson. Into these few short stanzas he put a mountain of his truth; where there was leisure for grief, there was little fiction.

The Meaning of *Dr Zhivago*

> ... facts don't exist until man puts into them something of his own, some measure of his own wilful, human genius—of fairy tale, of myth.
>
> —Dr Zhivago

> All that flames upon the night
> Man's own resinous heart has fed.
>
> —W. B. Yeats

When a major poet, towards the end of his life, decides to break out in a completely new direction by writing a novel, and a long and ambitious novel at that, there is reasonable ground for surprise and curiosity. That T. S. Eliot, or Paul Valéry, should have published an immense novel in his sixties is hardly imaginable. That Pasternak should do so was equally unimaginable, until he did it. Like Eliot and Valéry, he was a distinguished member of the second generation of Symbolist poets, that generation who were born in the late nineteenth century and revealed their gifts before 1914. Pasternak's importance in the European Symbolist movement was well recognized in every country in which that movement flourished. In England, his poetry was the subject of important essays by C. M. Bowra (*The Creative Experiment*, 1949) and C. L. Wrenn (*Oxford Slavonic Papers*, Vol. II, 1951). In Russia, the Symbolist movement was frowned on by the Soviet authorities, and many of its most distinguished practitioners were silenced, executed or driven to suicide. Just as one of the historical functions of the Roman Empire was to make martyrs for Christianity, so one of the historical functions of the Soviet empire was to make martyrs for Symbolism. The parallel is not a frivolous one, for Symbolism was not merely a strategy for writing poetry but an attitude towards experience.

It was the last great concerted impulse in European letters; it died with Pasternak, and it left a hole that has never been filled.

Symbolist writing often uses exact description, but it is, nevertheless, basically anti-realistic. Where the realist holds that his duty is to reproduce faithfully the outer surface of life, in the belief that the inner essence will accumulate behind it just as it does in actual experience, the Symbolist is akin to the religious mystic in believing that the surface of life is a mere carapace, that truth is essentially mysterious and can be glimpsed only at moments of vision. It is the function of Symbolist writing to induce these moments of vision, which it does by intense meditation on symbols which are not symbols *of* anything that can be produced and named, but rather instruments for bringing the mind to an awareness of things that cannot be apprehended except by the intensely meditated symbol. Hence the 'epiphanies' of Joyce, hence the 'image' of the Imagists, hence the consistent refusal of poets of the Symbolist wing to provide 'explanations' of their poems or even to confirm or deny these explanations when produced by others.

Within this framework, Pasternak's work as a poet was well enough grasped and understood. Some of its qualities even came over in translation, and his reputation was international. What no one knew, all this time, was that Pasternak was one day to come before the world as a major, and perhaps the last, writer of the Symbolist novel; that he was not only the equal of Yeats or Rilke but also the equal of Joyce and Proust. His achievement thus over-arches modern literature and makes him arguably the greatest writer of the twentieth century. I say 'arguably' because, not knowing Russian, I cannot argue it myself. I read Pasternak in translation, and though I realize that this is unfortunate, it is consoling to recall that this is how the great Russian writers have always made their impact on the outside world. The tiny minority of non-Russians who can read Russian have done an invaluable job of bridge-building; but they, by themselves, would not have accounted for the great influence on humanity in general of Turgenev, Tolstoy, Dostoevsky, Chekhov and, more recently, Pasternak. If we have no Russian we cannot, of course, set up as critics of these writers, since criticism involves the ability to make a total response. But that should not stop us from acknowledging their influence and describing what seems to us the main import of their work. In the case of *Dr Zhivago*, this task is the more urgent since, for various non-literary reasons, it cannot be attempted in the country in which the book was written, and to whose scenes and peoples it refers.

I

An old Russian folk-song is like water in a weir. It looks as if it were still and were no longer flowing but in its depths it is ceaselessly rushing through the sluice-gates and its stillness is an illusion.

By every possible means—by repetitions and similes—it attempts to stop or to slow down the gradual unfolding of its theme, until it reaches some mysterious point, then it suddenly reveals itself. In this insane attempt to stop the flow of time, a sorrowful, self-restraining spirit finds its expression.

This description of Kubarikha's song (XII, 6) does not fit exactly the method of *Dr Zhivago*, but it certainly comes a good deal nearer than we should be likely to come if we started with conventional expectations based on the realistic novel. Pasternak was, it is clear, intensely interested in the novel as a form, especially in its still unexplored possibilities. But for the conventional rules and regulations of the novel, as developed over the last two hundred years, he seems to have felt a certain genial contempt. Most novelists have been studious of probability; Pasternak goes out of his way to introduce walloping coincidences. Most novelists keep their narrative fairly tidy, with large events in the foreground and small in the background; Pasternak will spend pages over a description of the weather, and bundle some major event into a couple of paragraphs (e.g., VI, 6).

Dr Zhivago is, however, a traditional, even an old-fashioned, novel in one important respect. It has a 'hero', a principal character whose thoughts and actions embody more or less exactly the values of the author. Even if we did not know a great deal about Pasternak from other sources, even if we did not have his other works and a record of many of his personal utterances, we should know that Yury Zhivago stands very close to Boris Pasternak; we should know it partly from the tone of the book itself, which is one of the very few major novels to make use of irony, and partly from the very important fact that Pasternak wrote, and published with the book, twenty-two poems supposed to be written by Zhivago, which are indistinguishable in tone, method and import from Pasternak's own mature work.

Dr Zhivago, then, has a hero whose values are substantially the author's, and whose experience embodies the lessons of the author's lifetime. Yury Zhivago is presented as a kind of Everyman; not a simple cardboard cut-out in peasant costume, but the kind of complex, all-suffering and all-knowing Everyman that Hamlet is, for instance. The word *zhivago* recalls the Russian words for *life*, *alive* and *living*; Edmund Wilson writes that in the old liturgical language of the Russian Church, this spelling is actually used for the adjective 'living' in its genitive and accusative forms. So that on the very first page of the book, when passers-by at the funeral ask who is being buried and are told 'Zhivago', the Russian reader understands at once that Life is being buried and prepares himself to await the Resurrection. Zhivago is Life; he embodies human consciousness in all its facets. Like Hamlet, he may be powerless to alter his destiny, but he is extremely sensitive in his awareness of it. Nothing escapes him and nothing leaves him unaffected. He is responsive to other people, to the physical world, to art, to history, to the whole shifting mass of human experience. It is natural that he should be shown as a poet, since the poet has traditionally made a virtue of his openness to miscellaneous experience, and it is also natural that he should cultivate the scientific way of looking at the world. He is a doctor with a special gift for diagnosis (an episode, specially designed to plant this, is provided in IV, 5). And diagnosis is the art of deducing the whole from a part.

The concern for wholeness, and the gift of divining it, are also the mark of Zhivago the poet, whose attitude to his art is bound up, as it must be, with his idea of human character and destiny. We find the first major statement of this in his speech to the suffering Anna Gromeko in III, 3. Anna is afraid of her approaching death, and Yury rises to the occasion by delivering, rather to his own surprise, an 'impromptu lecture' on the subject of life, death and immortality. Here is the central passage:

Resurrection.—In the crude form in which it is preached for the consolation of the weak, the idea doesn't appeal to me. I have always understood Christ's words about the living and the dead in a different sense. Where could you find room for all these hordes of people collected over thousands of years? The universe isn't big enough, God and good and meaning would be crowded out. They'd be crushed by all that greedy animal jostling.

But all the time life, always one and the same, always incomprehensibly keeping its identity, fills the universe and is renewed at every moment in innumerable combinations and metamorphoses. You are anxious about whether you will rise from the dead or not, but you have risen already—you rose from the dead when you were born and you didn't notice it. Will you feel pain? Do the tissues feel their disintegration? In other words, what will happen to your consciousness? But what is consciousness? Let's see. To try consciously to go to sleep is a sure way to have insomnia, to try to be conscious of one's own digestion is a sure way to upset the stomach. Consciousness is a poison when we apply it to ourselves. Consciousness is a beam of light directed outwards, it lights up the way ahead of us so that we don't trip up. It's like the headlamps on a railway engine—if you turned the beam inwards there would be a catastrophe.

So what will happen to your consciousness? *Your* consciousness, yours not anyone else's. Well, what are *you*? That's the crux of the matter. Let's try to find out. What is it about you that you have always known as yourself? What are you conscious of in yourself? Your kidneys? Your liver? Your blood vessels?—No. However far back you go in your memory, it is always in some external, active manifestation of yourself that you come across your identity—in the work of your hands, in your family, in other people. And now look. You in others are yourself, your soul. That is what you are. This is what your consciousness has breathed and lived on and enjoyed throughout your life. Your soul, your immortality, your life in others. And what now? You have always been in others and you will remain in others. And what does it matter to you if later on it is called your memory? This will be you—the you that enters the future and becomes a part of it.

And now one last point. There is nothing to worry about. There is no death. Death is not our department. But you mentioned talent —that's different, that's ours, that's at our disposal. And to be gifted in the widest and highest sense is to be gifted for life.

At first sight this looks like an activist doctrine resembling official Marxist and Communist attitudes to a human life. That we exist 'always in some external, active manifestation' of our identity, that 'consciousness is a poison when we apply it to ourselves', would meet with no dissent from official Soviet opinion, with its insistence on work and more work, its disapproval of psycho-analysis, its demand for objectivity and representationalism in art. Zhivago is quite willing to go along with such doctrines up to a point. He is no individualist, or at any rate not quite in our usual Western sense. He believes in 'the you that enters the future and becomes part of it'. A man's jealously guarded individuality, the little box of tricks and idiosyncrasies that set him apart from others, seems to him merely trivial. What is important is life, the one thing we all share, and the all-important thing.

Art, of course, is life: life in one of its most important manifestations. Jumping forward to IX, 4, we find Yury writing in his notebook, during that first period at Varykino, before the renewal of his relationship with Lara, when he is putting his thoughts in order and enjoying the quiet and solitude of rural life before his capture by the partisans, that art 'is not a category', that it is 'a principle which comes into every work of art', that it is in fact 'a hidden, secret part of content'.

He goes on:

There is no plurality in art. Primitive art, the art of Egypt, Greece, our own—it is all, I think, one and the same art throughout, an art which remains itself through thousands of years. You can call it an idea, a statement about life, so all-embracing that it can't be split up into separate words; and if there is so much as a particle of it in any work which includes other things as well, it outweighs all the other ingredients in significance and turns out to be the essence, the heart and soul of the work.

Art is like life in two important respects: it is 'so all-embracing that it can't be split up', and it is the seed of ferment, transfiguring the whole if it is present even in 'a particle'.

If we hold these two statements in focus we shall not be surprised, on turning to Zhivago's more formal statements on his art as a poet, to find that he sees the poet's role as impersonal. The poet goes where life leads him, and the leading-string is language. In XIV, 8, where he has his greatest burst of creative activity during that blessed interval of peace with Lara and her daughter, in the second period of Varykino, Zhivago is visited by 'inspiration'. The whole passage is crucial.

After two or three stanzas and several images by which he was himself astonished, his work took possession of him and he experienced the approach of what is called inspiration. At such moments the correlation of the forces controlling the artist is, as it were, stood on its head. The ascendancy is no longer with the artist or the state of mind which he is trying to express, but with language, his instrument of expression. Language, the home and dwelling of beauty and meaning, itself begins to think and speak for man and turns wholly into music, not in the sense of outward, audible sounds but by virtue of the power and momentum of its inward flow. Then, like the current of a mighty river polishing stones and turning wheels by its very movement, the flow of speech creates in passing, by the force of its own laws, rhyme and rhythm and countless other forms and formations, still more important and until now undiscovered, unconsidered and unnamed.

At such moments Yury felt that the main part of his work was not being done by him but by something which was above him and controlling him: the thought and poetry of the world as it was at that moment and as it would be in the future. He was controlled by the next step it was to take in the order of its historical development; and he felt himself to be only the pretext and the pivot setting it in motion.

Several important matters are dealt with here, briefly but

lucidly. The whole question of poetic form is illuminated not from the outside, as a matter of conventions, rules, working arrangements and external standards, but from the inside, as one more part of the great shaping activity that we know as language. Any work of literature is a collaboration between the individual writer and the nation that has forged the instrument of his language and put it into his hands, which is the reason why literature is more national than the other arts, and also why a people can take a more intimate pride in its great writers than in its great composers or painters or scientists; because they did part of the work themselves, they are right to feel proprietary about it. Language can 'think and speak for man' because he has, as we say nowadays, programmed it to do so; it is instinct with a life that man has breathed into it, and that life is capable of marvellous variations and extensions, among them poetic form and, for that matter, all other literary forms.

This absorption of the artist's individuality into the 'mighty river' of language is partly Pasternak's own variant of the traditional doctrine of poetic inspiration as we find it in Plato's *Ion*, and *passim* in western literature, and partly an extension of the basic idea that human fulfilment means diving into the life-giving current, going where the great impersonal forces lead you, rather than clinging on to the shreds and tatters of individuality. ('Talk to me of originality', said Yeats, 'and I will turn on you in fury.') One of the impersonal forces is certainly what the Marxist would call History. The 'thought and poetry of the world' is about to take the next step 'in the order of its historical development'. And we must assume that if Zhivago had not been writing poems, if fate had not granted him that interlude of threatened but perfect tranquillity in which his poetic genius might have its last and most joyful fling, then the essential work would still have been done by other poets here and there; the 'thought and poetry of the world' is an irresistible and impersonal force which will choose this or that individual to act through, but in any case cannot choose but act.

This view puts Pasternak squarely among those who believe that art is no mere icing on top of the cake, to be indulged in times of plenty but sternly omitted when more important matters claim priority; that it is, on the contrary, an elemental force, a condition of life as urgent as sex or hunger. From this it follows that an undue fastidiousness about technique, the relish of the 'formalist' for endless debate and agonizing choice among the competing ways and means of expression, is the mark of the minor artist, the dabbler through whom this mighty current does not flow strongly. If the 'mighty river' rolls strongly enough it cannot help polishing the stones; on the other hand, it will not stay to carve them into curious shapes. In his *Essay in Autobiography*, written about 1954, Pasternak gives his view of those artists who become preoccupied with 'experiment':

> Men who have died young, such as Andrey Bely and Khlebnikov, spent the last years of their lives looking for a new means of expression, dreaming of a new language, groping for its vowels, consonants and syllables.
>
> I have never understood the need for this kind of research. I believe the most astonishing discoveries of all to have been made at moments when the sense of his work so possessed the artist that it left him no time to think and he was driven by his urgency to speak new words in the old language, without stopping to know if it was old or new.

It all circles back to that sentence in Yury's 'impromptu lecture' to Anna: 'To be gifted in the highest and widest sense is to be gifted for life'. But this being 'gifted for life' does not involve the complete surrender of what we ordinarily think of as individuality. The artist's destiny is to surrender to the powers that move him, to speak with the voice of all humanity at the point of the historical process that has been reached. But he does this not by subscribing to some big general doctrine like Marxist-Leninism, but by simply and unselfconsciously accepting the things that happen to him as a person. Zhivago's poems, as we have them at the end of the book, are full of personal details, but even if we did not have them we should still know that this was his way of working, from the description in III, 17 of the thoughts that pass through Zhivago's head as he plans to write a poem in memory of Anna Ivanovna Gromeko.

> With joyful anticipation, he thought of the day or two which he would set aside and spend alone, away from the university and from his home in order to write a poem in memory of Anna. He would include in it all those random things which life would send his way—a few descriptions of Anna's best characteristics; Tonya in mourning; street incidents on the way back from the funeral; and the washing hanging in the place where he had wept as a child and the blizzard had raged.

There is no need for the poet to go out and gather material. As for accepting material handed to him from outside, that is out of the question. 'Life', not only the broad impersonal force but his own personal life, made up of details and cluttered with seeming irrelevances, will send him his material. But by submitting to life, he will switch on something as old, as new, as wide, as deep, as humanity.

II

As diagnostician, as poet, Zhivago's values are founded on the idea of wholeness. In the story, the people to whom he is opposed are always those whose aim it is to substitute a part for the whole, to freeze off everything in life except the part that happens to engage them. There is a whole gallery of such figures, from the deaf-mute Yury encounters in the train on his way back from Melyuzeyevo to Moscow (V, 14) to the partisan leader Liberius and, most notably of all, Pasha Antipov, husband of Lara, who accepts the values of the revolution so completely that he restructures his entire character and makes himself over into the metallic Strelnikov, 'the Shooter'. Antipov/Strelnikov is worth examining in detail. As a young boy, he is shown as quick, bright and affectionate, with a special gift for mimicry with which he amuses his foster-mother Tiverzina, on whose protection he is thrown when his father is arrested in the upheaval of 1905. Later, as a young man at the university, he is headlong in love with Lara and entirely dominated by her. It is his nature to twine round a stronger being. This results in a marriage-situation which does not quite make him happy, and he also finds life in a country province narrow and boring. Lara enjoys it, because she has that deep sanity and wholeness within herself that is nourished by the fruitful rhythms of nature and the interests of ordinary human beings. The war provides Pasha's answer by giving him an acceptable reason for leaving home and trying out his manhood. But the trial results in a complete and unforeseeable change. Just before he comes back into the story in the new and unrecognizable guise of Strelnikov, Pasternak halts the action to give us a dispassionate, objective summary of what has happened to him.

His father was a worker who had been sent to prison for taking part in the revolution of 1905. He did not himself participate in the revolutionary movement in those years, at first because he was too young, and later, at the university, because young men who come from a poor background value higher education more and work harder than the children of the rich. The ferment among other students left him unmoved. He accumulated an immense amount of information and, after taking his degree in arts, educated himself later in science and mathematics.

Exempted from the army, he enlisted as a volunteer, was commissioned, sent to the front, captured and, on hearing of the revolution in Russia, escaped in 1917 and came home. He had an unusual power of clear and logical reasoning, and he was endowed with great moral purity and sense of justice; he was ardent and honourable.

But to the task of a scientist breaking new ground, his mind would have failed to bring an intuition for the incalculable; the capacity for those unexpected discoveries which shatter the barren harmony of empty foresight.

And in order to do good to others he would have needed, besides the principles which filled his mind, an unprincipled heart—the kind of heart that knows of no general cases, but only of particular ones, and has the greatness of small actions.

Filled with the loftiest aspirations from his childhood, he had looked upon the world as a vast arena where everyone competed for perfection, keeping scrupulously to the rules. When he found that this was not a true picture, it did not occur to him that his conception of the world order might be over-simplified. He nursed his grievances and with them the ambition to judge between life and the dark forces which distort it, and to be life's champion avenger.

Embittered by his disappointment, he was armed for the revolution. (VII, 30)

No doubt Pasha's early gift for mimicry, his tendency to sink his own personality into something outside himself and stronger, points to an inner weakness which makes possible his later corruption by the poison of dogma, of schematic and partial thinking. Antipov is a brave and honourable man; his death, as we shall see later, is given the full tragic treatment in one of the book's finest passages. But for temperamental reasons, and also for reasons connected with the circumstances of his life, he falls victim to the spiritual scourge of dogmatism. This disease is diagnosed, and its effects noted, everywhere throughout the book. As Zhivago says, almost casually, in one of his conversations with the local fixer Samdevyatov :

'. . . You talk about Marxism and objectivity. I don't know any teaching more self-centred and further from the facts than Marxism. Ordinarily, people are anxious to test their theories in practice, to learn from experience, but those who wield power are so anxious to establish the myth of their own infallibility that they turn their back on truth as squarely as they can. Politics mean nothing to me. I don't like people who are indifferent to the truth.' (VIII, 4)

This doctrine of wholeness, of respect of the 'unprincipled' heart for the truth in all its complexity, is never more beautifully stated than in Lara's meditations, after Yury's death, on the nature of the love between them.

It was not out of necessity that they loved each other, 'enslaved by passion', as lovers are described. They loved each other because everything around them willed it, the trees and the clouds and the sky over their heads and the earth under their feet. Perhaps their surrounding world, the strangers they met in the street, the landscapes drawn up for them to see on their walks, the rooms in which they lived or met, were even more pleased with their love than they were themselves.

Well, of course, it had been just this that had united them and had made them so akin! Never, never, not even in their moments of richest and wildest happiness, had they lost the sense of what is highest and most ravishing—joy in the whole universe, its form, its beauty, the feeling of their own belonging to it, being part of it.

This compatibility of the whole was the breath of life to them. And consequently they were unattracted to the modern fashion of coddling man, exalting him above the rest of nature and worshipping him. A sociology built on this false premise and served up as politics, struck them as pathetically home-made and amateurish beyond their comprehension. (XV, 15)

III

Even in translation, one can see that the book's literary method is designed to express in every possible way this attitude, this reverence for the wholeness of life. The celebrated coincidences are primarily a way of reminding us of the extent to which our lives are woven in with other people's. The conventional novel avoids coincidences because it feels a need to demonstrate that character is destiny: or, alternatively (if it is that kind of novel) that social circumstances will shape a life inexorably. In either case, to allow chance into the story is to spoil the neatly ruled pattern. Pasternak delights in spoiling the pattern, or rather in opening it up to show the deeper pattern underneath. Since experience is indivisible, it does not flow unbrokenly from character nor from social circumstances. Chance plays just as large a part as anything else. It must have pleased him to begin the story with a large-scale coincidence; in Chapter I, the train that suddenly halts within earshot of Nikolai Nikolayovich, Yury, and Nicky Dudorov, and from which Yury's father has just thrown himself to his death, is carrying Komarovsky, Tiverzina, and Mischa Gordon and his father. Since Tiverzina is the foster-mother of Pasha Antipov, later to be the husband of Lara, the roll-call of the book's central characters is very nearly complete. Since life will in any case bring these people together, there is no need for Pasternak to contrive a situation in which they will be crowded on to the one canvas; he does so as a deliberate gesture away from realism and towards a symbolic presentation.

There are also a number of linking devices that bind the huge, episodic narrative into a unity. Sometimes these are almost Joycean in the feeling of circularity they create. The most obvious example is that Komarovsky brings Lara into Yury's life and in the end takes her out again. Equally important is the candle that burns in the window of Pasha Antipov's apartment in Kamerger Street (III, 9, 10). Lara, whose engagement to Pasha has been on and off several times, impulsively calls on him and tells him they must be married immediately. She is highly distressed, being on her way to that party at which she will shoot at Komarovsky, miss him and hit someone else, and in an effort to regain calm she asks him to light a candle and put out the electric light. He does so, and as the candle stands in the window it melts the thick frost and makes 'a black chink like a peep-hole'. Just then, Yury and Tonya drive past, on their way to the same party, and Yury notices the hole. 'Its light seemed to fall into the street as deliberately as a glance, as if the flame were keeping a watch on the passing carriages and waiting for someone.' Yury and Tonya have just allowed the dying Anna to 'betrothe' them; at the Sventitsky's party, Yury will see Lara for the second time. This crucial point of inter-section is also the theme of Zhivago's poem 'Winter Night'. And finally, this very room is the poet's last resting-place; Yevgraf hires it for him in his last attempt to bring some peace and order into his life and set him on his feet, and after Yury dies he is laid out, and Lara's great lyrical outburst of joy and grief is uttered over his body, in this room where the candle had shone.

Apart from such large examples, there are many unobtrusive threads stitched into the larger design which tend to pull it towards a centre. In III, 1, Markel the handyman comes to help Anna Gromeko with a large wardrobe, a present from her husband; it has had to be carried upstairs piecemeal, and all the time Markel is reassembling it his six-year-old daughter, Marinka, is sucking barley-sugar and watching. Anna's pulmonary weakness, which later brings on her death, is related to a fall she takes while clumsily trying to help Markel. Years later, when Yury has parted from both Tonya and Lara and drifted back to Moscow, he lives in the same building as Markel and his wife, and Marinka, known now by her grown-up name of Marina, becomes his third consort. Again, there is the old Swiss lady, Mlle Fleury, the pensioned-off governess of the aristocratic family who used to own the house that is now run as a hospital, in Melyuzeyevo, to which Yury is assigned during his war service. Mademoiselle, who is described as 'steeped in the love of passionate intrigue so dear to the Latin heart', witnesses the beginning of the love of Yury and Lara, and perhaps even helps to nudge it into motion by her unshakeable conviction that 'the nurse and the doctor were bound to be attracted to one another'. After Yury leaves Melyuzeyevo, Mlle Fleury disappears from the action and is completely forgotten. But when Yury is dying, when his heart gives out on the crowded tram, an old lady is trudging along the pavement, fanning herself and almost overcome by the summer heat. Since she and the tram are going in the same direction, and the tram has a defective motor which keeps breaking down, they keep overtaking one another and the old, shuffling figure, whom he does not recognize, comes repeatedly into Yury's field of vision.

Yury thought of the conundrums in school arithmetic, in which you are asked how soon and in what order trains, starting at different times and going at different speeds, arrive at their destination; he tried to remember the general method of solving them, but it escaped him, and he went on from these school memories to others, and to still more complicated speculations.

He thought of several people whose lives run parallel and close together but at different speeds, and wondered in what circumstances some of them would overtake and survive others. Something like a theory of relativity applied to a human racecourse occurred to him, but he got completely muddled and gave it up.

There was a flash of lightning and a roll of thunder. The luckless tram was stuck for the twentieth time; it had stopped half-way down the hill from Kudrinsky Street to the Zoo. The lady in lilac appeared in the window-frame, passed beyond it and moved on.

The first heavy drops of rain fell on the roadway, the pavement and the lady. A gusty wind whipped past the trees, flapped the leaves, gave a tug at the lady's hat, turned up the hem of her skirt and suddenly died down.

... By an inhuman effort of the will, Yury pushed through the solid crowd down the gangway, swaying and stumbling, and came out on the rear platform; people blocked his way and snapped at him. The fresh air seemed to revive him and he thought that perhaps not everything was lost, perhaps he was better.

He began to squeeze his way through the crush on the rear platform, provoking more snarls, curses and kicks. He paid no attention to them, tore himself free of the crowd, climbed down from the stationary tram into the roadway, took a step, another, a third, fell down on the cobbles and did not get up again.

There arose a hubbub of talk, arguments, advice. Several people got off the tram and surrounded him. They soon ascertained that he was no longer breathing: his heart had stopped. The group round the body was joined by others who stepped off the pavements, some relieved and others disappointed that the dead man had not been run over and that his death had nothing to do with the tram. The crowd grew larger. The lady in lilac came up, too, stood a little, looked at the body, listened to the talk and went on. She was a foreigner, but she understood that some people were in favour of putting the body on the tram and taking it to the hospital, while others said that the militia should be called at once. She did not wait to see the outcome.

The lady in lilac was a Swiss national, she was Mademoiselle Fleury from Melyuzeyevo, and was by now very, very old. For twelve years she had been writing to the authorities in Moscow for permission to return to her native country, and quite recently her application had been granted. She had come to Moscow for her exit visa and was now on the way to her embassy to collect it, fanning herself as she went with her documents, which were done up in a bundle and tied with a ribbon. So she walked on, overtaking the tram for the tenth time, and quite unaware that she had overtaken Zhivago and survived him. (XV, 12)

When Yury, 'by an inhuman effort of the will', fights his way to the door and throws himself off the tram, to die on the pavement, this too is a linking device; his father, in the opening chapter, has died by throwing himself off a train.

Everywhere the narrative is criss-crossed by these linking devices. With the inexorable logic of a dream, the characters crop up and meet each other in different circumstances and guises. Pamphil, the brutalized infantryman whose bloodthirsty zeal for the revolutionary war has earned him much honour, but who is unhinged and needs Zhivago's medical attention in the Partisan camp, and finally dismembers his family with an axe, turns out to have fired the shot that killed the idealistic young commissar Gintz in a much earlier phase (V, 10). Terenty Galuzin, the lad just about to be conscripted in Admiral Kolchak's forces, who takes to the forest rather than wait to be involved in reprisals for a bomb outrage about which he knew nothing, turns up in the Partisans' camp; here, he is once again the victim of reprisals, falls wounded before a firing-squad, lies under the corpses and then escapes back to the forest. Later, seeking to amass revolutionary merit to save the life of his mother, held as a hostage, Terenty meets Strelnikov, now a fugitive, and wins his confidence and then betrays him to the Cheka. Another boy, Vassya Brykin, is press-ganged in Petersburg and put on a train for Siberia, where he meets Zhivago and his family on their way to Varykino. Years later, when his adventures are over, Yury is making his way on foot across the country when Vassya suddenly appears and recognizes him. They make their way to Moscow and share lodgings for some years.

The imagery of the book also makes a steady and all-pervading contribution to the novel's insistent suggestion that life is indivisible, that there are not different kinds of life but only life and not-life. We first meet Nicky Dudorov (I, 8) as the imaginative boy who is possessed by the thought of a certain tree that grows in the courtyard of a house in Tiflis where he is taken for holidays. The tree is 'a clumsy, tropical giant, with leaves like elephants' ears which sheltered the yard from the scorching southern sky. Nicky could not get used to the idea that it was a plant and not an animal.' A little earlier we have had the simile of the sun, with its level evening rays, coming to look at the body of the suicide Zhivago as it lies beside the railway line, 'like a cow from a near-by herd come to take a look at the crowd'.

The small town of Melyuzeyevo, on a summer night, furnishes a cluster of these barrier-crumbling similes:

> Narrow, dead-end streets ran off the square, as deep in mud as country lanes and lined with crooked little houses. Fences of plaited willow stuck out of the mud like the tops of lobster pots. You could see the one-eyed glint of open windows. From the small front gardens, sweaty yellow heads of maize with oily whiskers looked in at the windows, and single pale thin hollyhocks gazed into the distance over the fences, like women in their night-shifts whom the heat indoors had driven out for a breath of air. (V, 7)

Even physical impressions are deliberately scrambled. The sound of church bells on Maundy Thursday sinks through the drizzle-heavy air 'as a clump of earth, torn from the river bed, sinks and dissolves in the water of the spring floods' (X, 3): an image that connects the religious festival with the natural rhythm of the seasons.

But Pasternak's method is far more complex than these random samplings would indicate. His English translators have been forced to simplify a good deal, but even in what remains we can see a densely woven texture which can only be described by analysing fairly closely a specimen passage.

Let us take as our example the way Pasternak uses the image of the rowan tree and its scarlet berries. This image is used most frequently in Chapter XII, to which it gives the title, 'Iced Rowanberries'. Yury is in captivity with the partisans, and just outside the camp stands a 'splendid, solitary, rusty rowan'.

> Growing on a mound which rose above the low, sucking, hummocky marsh, it reached into the sky, holding up the flat round shields of its hard crimson berries against the leaden menace of winter. Small winter birds with feathers as bright as frosty dawns—bullfinches and tom-tits—settled on it and picked the largest berries, stretching out their necks and throwing back their heads to swallow them.

There seemed to be a close living connection between the birds and the tree, as if the rowan had watched them for a long time, refusing to do anything, but had in the end had pity on them: as though, like a foster mother, she had unbuttoned herself and offered them her breast, smiling as much as to say: 'Well, all right, all right, eat me, have your fill.' (XII, 1)

The first connection is established; the tree is like a foster-mother, indifferent at first, but yielding to entreaties and giving sustenance from her generous nipples.

Some days later, Yury overhears the peasant woman Kubarikha singing her folk-song. This woman, who has come with the influx of women and children when the partisans insist on having their families with them, is a kind of witch-doctor, very stubborn and backward, exactly the kind of person disapproved of by the régime. She claims magical powers and speaks in wild, poetic images. ('That whirlwind isn't just wind and snow, it's a were-wolf, a changeling that's lost its little warlock child and is looking for it—it goes about the fields crying and looking for it.') She is, predictably, contemptuous of the new politics and calls the red flag 'the purple kerchief of the death woman'. The song she sings, not knowing that she is overheard, is like a blend of an old Russian folk-song and a Symbolist poem. It begins with a hare running across a snowy field past a rowan tree, but before long the speaker becomes unmistakably human and towards the end identifies himself as 'a soldier' in 'captivity'.

> 'As a hare was running about the wide world,
> About the wide world, over the white snow,
> He ran, the lop-eared hare, past a rowan tree,
> Past a rowan tree and complained to her:
> Have I not, I—lop-eared hare, a timorous heart,
> Frightened of the wild beast's tracks,
> The wild beast's tracks, the wild wolf's hungry belly.
> Pity me, O rowan bush! O fair rowan tree!
> Do not give thy beauty to the wicked enemy,
> The wicked enemy, the wicked raven.
> Scatter thy red berries to the wind,

> Scatter them in handfuls to the wind, and let it carry them
> Over the wide world, over the white snow.
> Fling them, roll them to my native town,
> To the far end of the street, the last house,
> The last house in the street, the last window, the room
> Where she hides in hermit solitude,
> My dear, my longed for love.
> Whisper to my grieving love, my bride,
> A warm, an ardent word.
> I, a soldier, languish in captivity,
> Homesick, I—poor soldier, kept in foreign parts.
> I'll escape out of my bitter durance,
> I will go to my red berry, my fair love.'

The rowanberries are the bounty of nature, including love; the tree is beseeched not to give them to the cruel and wicked who deny life, but to scatter them freely to everyone else, and in particular for the woman he longs for. By the last line, this woman has herself become 'my red berry, my fair love'.

A little later, Yury is present when Kubarikha performs an exorcism on a barren cow. The sybil is a figure of majesty, despite her incongruous dress and physical decay; her 'haughty and passionate expression' gives to her eyes 'a youthful darkness and fire'. She ends her ritual with a catalogue of magical events.

> 'And many other things there are, such as stones raining from heaven, so that a man may go forth out of his house and the stones rain upon him. Or, as some have seen, horsemen riding through the sky, the horses' hooves hitting the tops of the houses. Or as sorcerers prophesied of old, saying: "In this woman there is corn, in that one honey, in a third pine-marten." And the knight opened the shoulder of the woman, as if it were a casket, and with his sword he took out of her shoulder-blade a measure of corn or a squirrel or a honeycomb.'

Pasternak immediately adds the reflection:

> No deep and strong feeling, such as we may come across here and there in the world, is unmixed with compassion. The more we

love the more the object of our love seems to us to be a victim. Occasionally, a man's compassion for a woman exceeds all measure, and his imagination removes her from the realm of possible happenings and places her in situations which are never encountered in life. He sees her at the mercy of the surrounding air, of the laws of nature and of the centuries which preceded her.

Yury was sufficiently well read to realize that Kubarikha's last words had been the opening passage of an ancient chronicle, either of Novgorod or Ipatyevo, but so distorted by the errors of copyists and the repetitions of sorcerers and bards that its original meaning had been lost. Why then should the nonsensical images thus handed down have gripped and moved him with the force of real events?

. . . Lara's left shoulder was half open. Like a key turning in the lock of a secret safe, the sword unlocked her shoulder-blade and, opening the cavity of her soul, revealed the secrets she kept in it. Memories of strange towns, streets, rooms, countrysides, unrolled like a film, like a skein, a bundle of skeins of ribbons tumbling out.

How well he loved her, and how lovable she was, in exactly the way he had always thought and dreamed and needed. Yet what was it that made her so lovely? Was it something that could be named and singled out in a list of qualities? A thousand times no! She was lovely by virtue of the matchlessly simple and swift line which the Creator at a single stroke had drawn round her, and in this divine outline she had been handed over, like a child tightly wound up in a sheet after its bath, into the keeping of his soul.

All these passages are woven into a seamless fabric. Why do the distorted passages from the old chronicle, the 'nonsensical images' resulting from the corruptions of bards and copyists, grip and move Yury with the force 'of real events'? The answer is given in the preceding paragraph. If the beloved woman is always seen through the vision of a compassionate imagination, at the mercy of the surrounding air and of the centuries that preceded her, if like a burning-glass she draws all experience and memory to one single spot, then part of what affects her, and determines her destiny, is precisely that amalgam of dream and experience, memory and imagination, which made the old bards alter the chronicle into a shape that was 'nonsensical' and yet 'gripped' Yury's mind. Kubarikha, no less than Zhivago though on a more primitive and shadowy level, stands for life and wholeness; she is like Madame Sosostris in *The Waste Land*, in that what she says in detail may be mere superstition but has an intuition underneath it which is recognized by the other inhabitants as a wisdom lacking in themselves; Madame Sosostris knows that death by drowning is more to be feared than death on land, and Kubarikha knows that 'you have to know everything—bidding and forbidding, the word for escaping and the word for safe-keeping'.

Immediately after the supremely beautiful image of Lara as a child wrapped tenderly in a bath-towel, given into his soul's keeping, Yury has his mystical vision of the head of Christ. And the voice that falls on his ears is Kubarikha's: 'Pray to the Mother of God who is the abode of light and the book of the living word.'

The witch has her own *pietas* which is subordinate to, not in conflict with, the love of God. And the image of the rowan-berry tree, in her song, is entwined with the image of Lara, who is the living force of life, nature and love. Yury's love for Tonya and his children by her is also very strong in him, and his decision to escape from the partisans is taken after an agonizing stab of grief for her (XII, 9). He gets past the sentry by saying that he wants to pick some berries from the rowan tree; the sentry mocks this piece of gentry's folly but contemptuously allows him to pass (the values represented by the rowan are opaque to the world of power and coercion). The chapter ends with a strong invocation of the tree's image:

> The footpath brought Yury to the foot of the rowan whose name he had just invoked.
>
> It was covered half in snow, half in frozen leaves and berries and it held out two white branches welcomingly. He remembered Lara's strong white arms and seized the branches and pulled them to him. As if in answer, the tree shook snow all over him. He muttered senselessly:
>
> 'I'll find you, my beauty, my love, my rowan tree, my own flesh and blood.'
>
> It was a clear night with a full moon. He made his way further

into the *tayga*, to the marked tree, dug his things out and left the camp.

We have not quite finished with this image. It stays in our minds, and recurs at the end of the most moving, and in many ways the central, chapter in the book, 'Again Varykino'. There, after the terrible ordeal of his parting from Lara—virtually the ending of his life, for afterwards he does no more than exist—Yury is visited by Pasha Antipov, *alias* Strelnikov, now broken and a fugitive. The two men talk of Lara and of their love for her. It is this chapter, presumably, that earned one critic's description of *Dr Zhivago* as 'the most profound description of love in all modern literature', a judgment with which one can only agree. In the morning Yury goes out to find that Pasha has shot himself in the yard, and that 'drops of blood which had spurted away and rolled in the snow made beads like iced rowanberries'.

It is impossible to unpack this last image. In a sense, the whole book is there. Once more we are reminded that we are reading a novel written by a great Symbolist poet. If William Shakespeare had lived in our time, a fate which he was fortunately spared, and had written a novel, I feel that this is the kind of novel it would have been. I am speaking subjectively, but not merely guessing at random, for after all Pasternak spent years working over Shakespeare as a translator and it can be shown that the two men had imaginative powers of much the same kind.

IV

I referred earlier to the 'mythopoetic density' of Symbolist writing. The clearest example of this is Joyce's use of the story of Odysseus as a back projection behind Mr Bloom's day in Dublin. Joyce pegs foregound to background in such a way that the random events of a day in the life of a salesman of advertising space become associated in our minds with the heroic adventures of Ulysses. There is no need to unpack this into a simple formula such as 'All human lives are equally important to the people who live them.' Bloom's unremarkable life takes on dignity by the implied comparison with Odysseus. But the Homeric story is also illuminated. Odysseus, Menelaus, Nausicaa, Penelope, are important because they share our common humanity. If human life is ennobled by the presence of high legend, the legend itself is revitalized; its human truth is confirmed.

It has frequently been noted that *Dr Zhivago* uses the New Testament in the same way that *Ulysses* uses the Odyssey. It is the screen on which the characters cast the giant shadows of their mythical dimension. But there the similarity ends. *Ulysses* is neat, logical, pegged out with the strong rational control that was Joyce's gift from his Jesuit education. *Dr Zhivago* uses the mythical dimension in a much more fleeting, tangential, multi-faceted, ungraspable way. Where Joyce is constructing a formal shadow play, Pasternak is lighting a row of tapers and letting them cast multiple, flickering, persistent shadows, always changing shape before our eyes but never disappearing altogether.

Thus to say that Zhivago 'is' Christ would be absurd, even in the unfixable way in which Leopold Bloom 'is' Odysseus. Pasternak's method does not allow figure-for-figure identification at any point, though it is clear that Lara has some elements of Mary Magdalene and Komarovsky of Judas. The New Testament background to Zhivago's story is purposely made both vague and more all-pervading. They are alike in their central metaphors, in their atmosphere of poignancy and exaltation, of high tragedy seen against a dawning sky.

I do not know what was Pasternak's attitude to Christianity, but the attitude he gives to Zhivago is that the teachings of Christ were the greatest moral break-through in human history. Men are defined by what they choose to worship. Whether or not Christ was the Son of God, whether or not He actually said, 'Father, forgive them, for they know not what they do' as He hung on the cross, it was a break-through for humanity that men should believe these things and that they should use them to project their idea of the highest reach of moral beauty and courage, the ultimate good which deserved to be worshipped. If we compare that supreme moment of the Christian story with anything in the Graeco-Roman tradition, we see at once the tremendous stride that humanity had taken, even if the Christian religion contained no revelation and was simply a human fabrication.

I am not one of those who claim to have settled this question, and in those last few sentences I was giving my own opinion. But it is also the opinion that we find in *Dr Zhivago*. As early as I, 5 we find Nikolai Nikolayovich giving a long and passionate exposition of the view that human history begins with Christ. 'What you don't understand', he says to the uncomprehending social philosopher Ivan Ivanovitch, 'is that it is possible to be an atheist, it is possible not to know if God exists or why He should, and yet to believe that man does not live in a state of nature but in history, and that history as we know it now began with Christ, it was founded by Him on the Gospels.'

Nikolai Nikolayovich is an important character who fades out half-way through the story because there is no further need for him. His function is partly to act as an awakening influence on the young Zhivago's mind, rather as the composer Scriabin did on the young Pasternak's, and partly to have a mature character who can begin at once to voice the book's essential doctrine. It is one of the marks of Pasternak's indifference to conventional novelistic practice that he never shrinks from undramatized exposition of ideas; the book makes its points by the purest poetic means of suggestion and symbol, but also, when the author happens to feel like it, by great chunks of overt exposition. Undoubtedly the most important of these is in XIII, 17, when Yury and Lara are living in Yuryatin. A female character, Sima Tuntseva, is brought in solely in order to visit them and deliver a long discourse. Yury lies on the sofa in the next room, and listens through the open door; Lara, picking up her sewing, remarks: 'I like to listen to a long, wise discourse when it's snowing . . . Go on, Sima dear. I'm listening.'

Sima then states one of the most important of the book's sustaining ideas.

'I don't like such words as "culture" and "epoch". They are

confusing. I prefer to put it another way. As I see it, man is made up of two parts, of God and work. Each succeeding stage in the development of the human spirit is marked by the achievement over many generations of an enormously slow and lengthy work. Such a work was Egypt. Greece was another. The theology of the Old Testament prophets was a third. The last in time, not so far replaced by anything else and still being achieved by all that is inspired in our time, is Christianity.'

She goes on to elaborate on this idea in a statement running to three pages, not a word of which should be lost by the attentive reader. ('Of course, she's taken it all from Uncle Kolya's books,' Yury thinks to himself.) The change in humanity that came with a changed idea of the divine, the suddenness with which 'the reign of numbers was at an end' and 'the story of a human life became the life story of God and filled the universe', leads Sima to the beautiful meditation on the figure of Mary Magdalene. 'What familiarity, what equal terms between God and life, God and the individual, God and a woman!'

The pre-Christian idea of God was bound up with power in the obvious sense: masses, force, armies, nations. With Christ came the idea of divinity as individual self-realization, the unique soul flooded with light—in short, 'equal terms between God and life'. And Zhivago's disillusion with the thoughts and feelings of the post-revolutionary régime arises from the fact that these *exaltés* have turned the clock back, turned away from the idea of the free individual spirit and gone back to thinking in terms of masses, nations, vast general movements governed by theories, so that when the revolutionary attitudes have hardened into dogma he can look back sadly on the early days when 'everyone had gone mad in his own way' (XIV, 14). What distinguishes Christ from earlier and cruder notions of God is precisely that Christ does not impose His will on life from the outside, but on the contrary submits to it. The object of Christian worship is a God who says to mankind: 'I will not thump you into submission to my will; far from it, I will suffer every humiliation and agony you can heap on me, and still emerge as a God, with my radiance undimmed by what you have done to me and to yourselves.' And Christ does this without pomp, modestly, unobtrusively, almost without volition, merely by being true to His nature.

Zhivago's poem 'Hamlet' is relevant here. It will be convenient to have it on the page:

> The noise is stilled. I come out on the stage.
> Leaning against the door-post
> I try to guess from the distant echo
> What is to happen in my lifetime.
>
> The darkness of night is aimed at me
> Along the sights of a thousand opera-glasses.
> Abba, Father, if it be possible,
> Let this cup pass from me.
>
> I love your stubborn purpose,
> I consent to play my part.
> But now a different drama is being acted;
> For this once let me be.
>
> Yet the order of the acts is planned
> And the end of the way inescapable.
> I am alone; all drowns in the Pharisees' hypocrisy.
> To live your life is not as simple as to cross a field.

True to Symbolist practice, the poem works through a multiple consciousness: the central figure is Hamlet, and also an actor playing Hamlet, and also Christ. (If we add 'and also Zhivago', this need not involve us in any crude over-literalness.) The actor has to nerve himself to face the audience; Hamlet has to face the tragic fact of his responsibility to the situation, the 'cursed spite' that he was 'born to set it right'; Christ wishes it were possible to 'let this cup pass from me', but knows that His destiny is what it is. The last line, as the translators explain, is a proverb: this has the effect of landing the poem squarely in the lap of the ordinary human reader who is neither tragic personage, actor, or God, but must bear some part of all three just by living a human life. In an essay commenting on his own translation of *Hamlet*, published in *Literaturnaya Moskva* in 1956, Pasternak remarked that the fact that Hamlet's command came to him through a ghost was not important. What matters is that 'by the merest accident Hamlet should be chosen to sit in judgment on his time and become the servant of a remoter one'. Hamlet was put into his tragic position by the 'accident' of being the king's son, otherwise he could have lived the studious private life that would have made him happy. But Hamlet accepted this as his fate and did not struggle against it. Turning back to the novel, this should help to make clear what has puzzled some readers, especially in England where there are so many Boy Scouts: why does Zhivago make so little effort to resist his fate, why does he go down, accepting a long period of decline before his death, suffering himself to be robbed of everything that made life worth living? Why does he not accept Komarovsky's offer to get him away to Vladivostok and thence out of Russia altogether? Why does he make no effort to escape when, at Varykino, he is in constant danger of arrest and execution?

The answer to this is, *mutatis mutandis*, the same as the answer to the similar questions about Hamlet (who didn't abdicate) and Christ (who didn't come down from the Cross). To be truly human, to be 'gifted in the highest and fullest sense', which means also to be truly divine, is to accept what life brings, to play out the role assigned to you, without trying to escape. Compare Zhivago's outburst to Liberius (XI, 5) about the folly of trying to reshape life:

'Reshaping life! People who can say that have never understood a thing about life—they have never felt its breath, its heart—however much they have seen or done. They look on it as a lump of raw material which needs to be processed by them, to be ennobled by their touch. But life is never a material, a substance to be moulded. If you want to know, life is the principle of self-renewal, it is constantly renewing and remaking and changing and transfiguring itself, it is infinitely beyond your or my inept theories about it.'

Zhivago's poems are full of this idea. 'March', for instance, with its marvellous evocation of spring ('That strapping dairy-maid'), ends with the lines

> The culprit and the life-giver
> Is the dung with its smell of fresh air.

When the poem first appeared in a periodical, the reference to dung as the cause of life and growth was cut out; Stalin had recently died, and no doubt the editor felt it was no time to be making remarks about life growing out of death—a good example of the caution which Soviet life makes necessary for literary men. Actually as we can see in a larger perspective, the theme of resurrection, the image of death fertilizing life, is always uppermost in Zhivago's mind, and in the mind of his creator.

The poem in which the idea of resurrection is most vividly present is not, oddly enough, among those which Zhivago actually wrote. He dreamed it during his attack of typhus (VI, 15) while his half-brother Yevgraf, the guardian and inspirer of his poetic self, came and went beside his bed.

> The subject of his poem was neither the entombment nor the resurrection but the days between; the title was 'Turmoil'.
>
> He had always wanted to describe how for three days the black, raging, worm-filled earth had assailed the deathless incarnation of love, storming it with rocks and rubble—as waves fly and leap at a sea coast, cover and submerge it—how for three days the black hurricane of earth raged, advancing and retreating.
>
> Two lines kept coming into his head :
>
> 'We are glad to be near you.'
> and
> 'Time to wake up.'
>
> Near him, touching him, were hell, corruption, dissolution, death; yet equally near him were the spring and Mary Magdalene and life.—And it was time to awake. Time to awake and to get up. Time to arise, time for the resurrection.

Finally, in what sense is Zhivago himself resurrected? The answer is given in the last words of the novel, 'it seemed that the book in their hands knew what they were feeling and gave them its support and confirmation'. Yury's two lifelong friends, Mischa Gordon and Nicky Dudorov, are sitting together at a high window, 'five or ten years' after Zhivago's death (such vagueness shows that the exact time doesn't matter), and turning over in their hands 'a book of Yury's writings which Yevgraf had compiled'. Yevgraf, whose name is associated with *ευ γραφει ν.* to write well, plays an entirely symbolic role in the action; he appears at those times when Yury is on the point of being submerged by his material worries and in desperate need of peace and order. Except for the supremely joyful but doomed interlude at Varykino in Chapter XIV, when Yevgraf's function was taken over by Lara, he has acted as the guardian angel of that side of Zhivago the creative artist. No attempt is made to explain how Yevgraf lives, where he goes to in between his sudden appearances, how he can always get food and accommodation, how he attains the rank of Major-General in the war; it is simply a *donnée.* That Yevgraf should collect Zhivago's scattered writings into a book (presumably a typescript, since there is no mention of its having been published or existing in more than one copy) is in keeping with his role, just as it is in keeping with the roles of Gordon and Dudorov that they should treasure the book and feel united in the impulse of joy that it brings them.

After all that has been said about the use of the New Testament as back-projection for *Dr Zhivago*, the reader will hardly miss the parallel between Yevgraf's compilation and the Gospels. All through the book, although Yury is shown as taking his vocation as a poet with complete seriousness, he never expresses any ambition to have a literary career or to transmit his work safely to posterity. Like Christ, he makes it his concern to express the truth and leaves to others the task of collecting and preserving what he utters. Gordon and Dudorov, though unalterably his friends, are conventional and rather stupid; even, at times, cowardly; very like the disciples of Christ as we glimpse them in the New Testament. In a moment of irritation during his last conversation with them, Yury thinks, 'Dear friends, how desperately commonplace you are . . . The only bright and living thing about you is that you are living at the same time as myself and are my friends.' In this conversation, too, he tells them of his approaching death. 'I'm not pretending, you know. It's an illness I've got, sclerosis of the heart. The walls of the heart muscle wear out and get too thin, and one fine day they'll burst.' The Bridegroom will not be with them much longer.

'Five or ten' years later—that is, within the era of Stalin, of blood, terror and injustice on an unheard-of scale—Gordon and Dudorov sit at the window and feel 'a peaceful joy for this holy city and for the whole land'. Objectively, there is little enough to warrant these stirrings of happiness. But then, five or ten years after the Crucifixion, the Roman Empire seemed as inert, as immovable, as brutal as ever.

Zhivago, like Christ, has triumphed by submitting. He has allowed material circumstances to sweep over him and then come sprouting up like the seed from the earth. Just as there are various points in the Gospel narrative at which Christ could have stepped aside from the path that led to the Cross, so there are various points in Zhivago's story at which he could have turned away from the years of decline, the descent into anonymity and poverty, the heart attack on the tram, the fatal spasm on the pavement. But he chose consistently to stay on that path. 'You have no will,' says Lara to him in one of their profound and tender conversations. But in the larger perspective of the whole story, we, the readers, can see that Zhivago does what a wilful man could not do. He builds his whole life on a deep act of choice, choosing his death and choosing his resurrection.

V

Of course I am far from claiming to understand everything in this great book; even allowing for the *nuances* which one misses in any translated work, there are some things that seem important but whose significance is not clear to me. In the last chapter, 'Epilogue', we are introduced to a girl named Tanya, an Army laundress, who is the daughter of Yury and Lara, born during the time Lara was with Komarovsky, and given away to be brought up by foster-parents; later, she became a *bezprizornaya*, one of the hordes of little waifs who roamed everywhere and were still a feature of Soviet life during the 1930s. Tanya tells a horrifying tale of how Petya, the crippled infant son of her foster-mother, was murdered in a cellar by some wandering ruffian who was himself summarily executed by the locals, who tied him to the railway line and drove a train over him. This episode would present no difficulty to those who read *Dr Zhivago* primarily as a social panorama; they would see it simply as an episode written to underline the brutal chaos of those years in Russia. The novel is certainly a social panorama among other things, and I would willingly interpret the episode in this way if it did not partake so much of the book's main stream of symbolism. Burial and re-emergence are such recurrent themes, all the way from Yury's poem about the Sepulchre to Terenty Galuzin's hiding under a pile of dead bodies and even to the importance, in a Siberian winter, of the proper method of digging a pit to store potatoes, that something important must hinge on the fact that the murder takes place underground and that the bandit kills the child as an act of revenge because the old mother is sitting on the trapdoor and will not let him out. But exactly what to read into it, I cannot decide.

Then there are the various elaborations of punning and word-play. These can only be worked on by a critic who can read Russian, but it is unlikely that they will be adequately dealt with by critics of Russian nationality, if only because the tradition of Russian criticism is socially orientated, deriving from such figures as Belinsky. Even if the Soviet Union should one day become sufficiently civilized to permit the free discussion of literature instead of its laborious exegesis on party lines, Russian critics would be unaccustomed to the kind of analysis that studies puns, textures, and allusions-within-allusions. The English-speaking world has had thirty years of practice on *Finnegan's Wake*, and this gives us a head start; *Dr Zhivago* had not been available for many months before Edmund Wilson, a critic whose normal approach is broadly social and biographical, was demonstrating what could be done by tracing the names of the characters back to their sources in the Russian Orthodox calendar and to mythology. Not content with the names, Mr Wilson went on to analyze some other details in the story and bring out their symbolism. The sign, 'Moreau and Vetchinkin. Seeders. Threshers', which occurs five times in the story, spurs him to a two-page analysis which I shall not attempt to summarize but which is worthy of William Empson or the more spirited of the 'New Critics' of twenty years ago. I don't know whether to be convinced by it, but there must be some significance in the sign, or why should it occur five times and at significant points in the story?

Mr Wilson's two essays on the book, 'Doctor Life and his Guardian Angel' and 'Legend and Symbol in *Doctor Zhivago*' are reprinted in his *The Bit Between My Teeth* (1966) and form, together, the best possible introduction. I found useful guide-lines in the chapter on Pasternak in F. D. Reeve's *The Russian Novel* (1966) and the essay by Frank Kermode in *Puzzles and Epiphanies* (1962). There is a good short study in French (*Pasternak*, by Guy de Mallac, Editions Universitaires, 1963). Max Hayward, in addition to his invaluable work as translator, has written an essay from which I learnt a great deal, though its point of view is not entirely the same as mine ('Pasternak's *Dr Zhivago*', *Encounter*, May 1958). Most illuminating of all, to me, is the compressed but intensely sympathetic study of the book in Henry Gifford's *The Novel in Russia* (1964), to which the seriously interested reader will add Mr Gifford's essay 'Pasternak and the "Realism" of Blok' (*Oxford Slavonic Papers*, XIII, 1967).

To apprehend and assimilate a great work of literature is essentially a corporate undertaking. Everybody adds his bit, and this is mine.

Interchapter

Thinking Russian

I HAVE been writing a long essay on Pasternak's *Dr Zhivago*, and now that it is finished and I ought to be turning to other things, I find that I cannot get Russia out of my head : not any particular aspect of the country or its people, but simply Russian-ness, the mass of impressions that comes into your mind if you say 'Russia' and close your eyes. I would gladly put this Russian-ness aside, having other work that urgently claims my attention, but I cannot. It is rather like the sensation of being haunted by a tune; I am not so much thinking about Russia, in the sense of looking objectively at facts and trying to assess them, as breathing in a Russian atmosphere that I cannot escape from because I am carrying it about with me.

I find this feeling described very well in an early essay of J. B. Priestley's ('A Fish in Bayswater', 1929). 'The stuff of which these things are made,' says Priestley, meaning these inward visions of another country, or landscape, or mode of being, 'comes out of our actual memories of real experiences and talks and books and art in general. Somebody says "France" to me, or I meet the word in some idle context, and immediately I see long straight roads, green shutters folded back, tables under trees, bearded citizens making their way to the café in the square, and all the rest of it. At least, that is how I am compelled to describe what happens, but actually I do not see a series of little pictures but somehow entertain a large confused idea that could be translated into these pictures and that gives me the feeling of having seen them.'

It is this 'large confused idea' of Russia that will not leave me. Russia, Russian-ness, the actual country as it is and has been, the ideas and books and people it has let loose on the world, are an enormous recurring fact in my consciousness. This is of course true of any country, and to carry about the 'large confused idea' of several other cultures is part of the experience of every man and woman, except a tiny minority of primitives who are entirely enclosed in their own five-mile square. (They probably compensate by focusing this square far more intently than we ever look at anything.)

Everyone, then, must have his own Russian thoughts, his own large confused idea, which comes into his consciousness when someone says 'Russia'. And since this kind of thing is a universal human experience, it falls within the writer's legitimate province.

I propose, then, to go back into my Russian reverie, and to take the reader, if he wishes, with me.

All bookish people get their first acquaintance with other countries, and with much in the life of their own country, from reading. In the case of Russia, this is a highly favourable introduction, for the Russian genius is particularly fertile in literature. In the nineteenth century their achievement is arguably the greatest in Europe, and from what one can make out round the edges of the censorship it is obvious that they are still a great literary nation, ready at any moment to assume a leading position if their ruling *cénacle* would only get off the writers' backs and let them be.

It hardly matters whether one comes to Russian literature early or late, so long as one comes to it. For instance, I was for years an admirer of Turgenev without knowing it. I admired, and still do, the short stories of Hemingway, especially those in which he combines an almost agonized sensitiveness to the sights and sounds, shapes and scents, of the natural world with a deep awareness, laconically conveyed, of the plight of the poor and unfortunate. A story like 'An Alpine Idyll', which begins with the lyrical description of springtime in the mountains and goes on, almost casually but with deadly effect, to convey the hard brutality of the peasant whose life has been formed by the struggle against the intractable Alps, came to me as a revelation. What I did not know at the time, and in fact waited twenty years to find out, was that the method of 'An Alpine Idyll' was fully developed by Turgenev in *A Sportsman's Sketches*, written in the late 1840s and early 50s.

What is more, Turgenev seems to accomplish so easily, with one hand almost, what it took Hemingway his whole strength to manage. And Hemingway's strength was very great.

The major Russian writers all share the refusal to be trammelled, the calm assumption that form is a matter of individual choice and that no reigning convention has any authority over them. It must be the gift of their vast stretches of wilderness, the enormous space between one town and another, between one circle of argufying critics and another—'the turkey-cock critics', Chekhov calls them—and its result is that the typical Russian master is a careless giant, inventing new forms as casually as he buttons his shirt.

Tolstoy, the chairman of Russian literature, was describing this side of the national genius when he said: 'I think every great artist necessarily creates his own form. If the content of works of art can be infinitely varied, so can their form. Once Turgenev and I came back from the theatre in Paris and discussed this. He completely agreed with me. We recalled all that is best in Russian literature and it seemed that in these works the form was perfectly original.'

If Western critics had borne these remarks of Tolstoy's in mind, they might not have been so unprepared for *Dr Zhivago*.

For us in western Europe, it must always be true that America and Russia inspire very similar feelings. They are both, to us, intensely *foreign* countries, in which human beings have contrived to build towns and establish a civilization in the face of constant discouragement from a difficult climate and immense distances. In both countries, this struggle to occupy and subdue the land has involved not only the fierce fight of man against nature but, perhaps as an inevitable side-effect, much fiendish cruelty of man to man. Both nations tolerated chattel slavery until the 1860s; both have always had, and still have today, immense numbers of the poor, the ignorant, and the forgotten, left behind as the top crust of the nation has moved steadily onward in power and wealth.

The word 'slave' comes from the medieval Latin *sclavus*, meaning a Slav; even then, Slavs tended to be slaves.

Negro emancipation did so little to make the Negroes happier, safer or more dignified that some of them even looked back with nostalgia on the days of their slavery. In just the same way, Firs in *The Cherry Orchard* speaks of the Emancipation of 1861 as 'the Troubles'.

The Soviet deportation of nationalities is paralleled by the dispossession of American Indians; the outbursts of cruelty, the pogroms with their flogging and knouting Cossacks, remind one of the hideous lynchings in the South; the concentration camps that have always existed in Russia, from Sakhalin Island about which Chekhov wrote such a harrowing report to the present-day Kolyma, described by one of its inmates as 'a cold Auschwitz of the north', have their counterpart in the Southern prison farms where the convicts are mainly Negroes; such places as Parchman penitentiary, in the Mississippi delta country south of Clarksdale, for example.

Both these vast countries are built on the bones of people who died like animals. Both fuel themselves by violence. How quaint English history must seem to them, with its tiny skirmishes and almost bloodless riots! At Peterloo, nine people died.

But these resemblances have not, after all, been sufficient to make the Russian and the American into cousins. Historical and racial differences, once thought trivial in comparison to environment, have asserted themselves. Edmund Wilson, writing in 1935, could feel, in those comparatively early Soviet days, that the landscape of Russia would mould the Russian political and social character and make it somehow like the American: that huge deep rivers, uncharted forests, illimitable steppes and prairies, would somehow do the job by themselves, now that the Russians had thrown off their landlords and abolished their aristocracy. It was a reasonable enough expectation, particularly since the 'line' had not yet hardened. The Russians, at that time, were highly suspicious of the West in general, but they had not yet developed any particular animus against Americans, whom they tended to admire for their energy and technical expertness. At that time, a good many American engineers were working on large Russian projects at the invitation of the Soviet government. When will an American engineer be invited to work in Russia again? Both the Rockies and the Urals will crumble to dust first.

Memories of a visit. I was in Russia, with my wife, for four weeks in 1960. In retrospect, these four weeks have expanded steadily until they now seem the equivalent of four years.

As a country to travel in, Russia has all the wonderful qualities I expected it to have. And those four weeks left my mind stored with images, not very different from the images I had already gathered from Russian literature, but for that very reason gliding easily in among them, and becoming entwined in a seamless fabric. Chekhov's house at Yalta has a tree growing in the courtyard; it is a quiet house, speaking of modest comfort and the carefully regulated life of an invalid. His bedroom is arranged as it was on the night of his death, though in fact he died far away from here, in Badenweiler. On that night, he was reading a medical journal before going to sleep; it is there, on the bedside table, and his slippers are by the bed. Pathetic, humbly useful slippers that kept warm the feet of Anton Chekhov! And his telephone on the wall: a long, elegant handle, delicately ribbed, with earpiece and mouthpiece sprouting from either end like delicate sea-shells. I hold it in my hand for a moment, and seem to hear his voice coming faintly over the line, as faintly as the sea's voice in a shell.

In the Caucasus, we went for a long, high walk one morning, and, pausing to rest on a bluff, saw a great golden eagle fly out over the mountainside, below us. I never expected to see an eagle from above. It is like seeing Chekhov's slippers—an unexpected perspective on a great natural force.

The tragedy is, of course, that one can so rarely be left in peace to enjoy these epiphanies. One cannot be an unofficial visitor—in Dickens's phrase, an Uncommercial Traveller—in Russia. In our case, we escaped the net of Intourist only to be caught in the even tighter mesh of the Soviet literary bureaucracy. They had published a book of mine; large funds in royalties had accumulated; nobody would give me a straight answer as to whether I could expect to get any of this money paid to me at home, but at least it would be available within the Soviet Union, and we were invited to go there and begin, at any rate, the pleasant task of spending it.

So, from the first, it was a matter of arrangements—letters back and forth, explanations and counter-explanations, beginning long before we arrived and going on all the time. In the end, I was so bethumped with arrangements that I came near to wishing I had never gone there, that I had cherished the idea of Russia in my mind, rich and dark and inexhaustible, like a Christmas cake that can be cut endlessly and will never grow stale. To pay an actual visit there is to have one's temper tried continually by arrangements with this person, arrangements with that organization, arrangements of every kind and of unbelievable complexity, and, since this is Russia, arrangements that invariably break down.

Well, almost invariably. Now and then, what we arranged actually happened. In Russia, nothing is entirely predictable; not even unpredictability.

My mind goes back to the first night of our arrival in Moscow. The arrangements, inevitably, were in a rich confusion from the start. In accordance with their usual literary custom, the Russians had published my book in a magazine, *Novy Mir*, before issuing it in book form. All my correspondence had been with the editorial offices of this magazine, who were thus my one link with the officialdom on which we were to be dependent for everything. How frail was this link, I had no idea. But it was in fact the case that the Union of Soviet Writers, and not *Novy Mir*, was in charge of us, and that it was the Union who had made, or rather failed to make, all the necessary arrangements.

Knowing nothing of this, we disembarked from the plane

(from Belgrade), looked around, saw no sign of being met, and cheerfully went to drink beer and eat caviar in the buffet, imagining that the question of accommodation could wait until we had refreshed ourselves and unpopped our ears. Meanwhile, a deputation of students, sent by Professor Valentina Evashova of Moscow University, had gone with flowers and prepared speeches of welcome to the wrong airport, on the other side of the city, and telephone calls were crackling back and forth from the offices of the Writers' Union.

Tranquil in our unawareness of all this, we finished our beer and caviar and went along to the Intourist office to ask about hotels. Here we waited in a queue behind (among others) a German who was trying to explain in English that he had made the acquaintance of an Englishwoman on the aeroplane and that they wanted to go to the same hotel for company. 'Can we sleep together?' he kept asking with perspiring innocence.

When it came to our turn, I explained to the man behind the desk, who was crouching defensively over an enormous ledger, that we had plenty of contacts in Moscow and that our only problem was the immediate one of finding a hotel for that night. He grunted warily and motioned us to stand on one side. Knowing what I know now, I have no doubt that he intended us to wait in a corner until the office closed, and then spend the night on a bench in the airport waiting-room. Being, as I was, still happy in my virgin ignorance of Russian ways, I moved aside contentedly enough. It was difficult, in any case, to feel anything very strongly. My sense of reality was impaired, as it always is by an air journey. The unreal sensation of being picked up in one country and deposited a few hours later in another, the deafness caused by flying in a light plane not insulated against pressure changes, the unfamiliarity of everything about me, and the sheer number of strange things that had happened since we had left home three months before, all combined with my fatigue, which was considerable, to produce a feeling of drunken complaisance. Smiling vaguely, I took my seat and prepared to wait.

At this moment my wife, who still had some grip on external

realities, chanced to hear through the open window the distant mumbling of a public-address system. It was impossible for her to tell what language the voice was using, and the sound was in any case coming from a remote part of the airport, but it seemed to her that the name 'Wain' occurred several times in the farrago of syllables. Alerted, she rose and sprinted out of the office, returning in a few minutes with the news that somebody wanted me on the telephone.

After that, all was action. I spoke, through a fusillade of crackles, to a man (in French), then to a woman (in English); I gathered that the Writers' Union was palpitating with anxiety to receive us; I was given directions, we found a taxi, and, after a drive that seemed to last half the night, we were reeling, festooned with luggage, into the lobby of the gigantic Hotel Sovietskaya, already twisting our faces into grateful smiles and looking round for our hosts.

The smiles dimmed again, for the vast lobby was deserted, and we set down our bags and waited. When nothing happened, we set off to find help. My ears popped and banged, but my deafness remained, and so did my sense of having wandered into a badly-directed film. No matter how sternly I told myself that all this was really happening, and happening *to me*, I could not convince myself that I was awake. We came upon a colossal desk, behind which sat a woman with the face of a labour-camp superintendent; this, we gathered, was the Administrator. I began to explain our situation to her, veering hopefully between English, French and mime, but she silently motioned me to hold my tongue, picked up the telephone, stared at it grimly for a moment, then dialled a number and began talking, quite obviously not about us.

Thirty minutes later, still deaf, still living in a dream, but beginning to feel a twinge of pity for the sufferings of my wife, who was still capable of normal human sensations of impatience and bewilderment, I was sitting in front of the Administrator's desk, watching her talk to her unguessable interlocutor, when I became aware of two figures slowly approaching us over the silent acreage of marble; a man of about my own age, and a small, plump, middle-aged woman. From the centre of my deaf somnolence I regarded them with idle benevolence. They went up to the Administrator, who continued stolidly to talk into the instrument, and addressed her. She disregarded them, but again the word 'Wain' fell on my ears, though from an immense distance. My wife was on her feet. These were our hosts.

A tumult of explanations broke out. The man, addressing me in French, began complaining that we had disorganized the arrangements of the Writers' Union by not keeping them informed. I explained that we had kept the editors of *Novy Mir* informed instead. He repeated what he had said before, perhaps thinking that I had not understood him. Then he smiled kindly and suggested that we should go to our room before dinner. As it was midnight, I found myself agreeable with him about going to our room, though not about dinner. I tried to explain this, and to the best of my knowledge I succeeded in explaining it. Nevertheless, fifteen minutes later we had deposited our luggage in a vast suite of rooms (normally reserved for ambassadors, but given to us as the only accommodation the hotel had left), and the four of us were in the restaurant, waiting to be served with dinner.

The rest of the night lives in my mind as an accelerating swirl of fatigue and confusion. The restaurant was of the huge old-fashioned type which the Russian mind associates with magnificence. A noisy dance-band was playing, a thing I do not care for at the best of times when I am trying to eat. We sat at a fairly large table, my wife and I on one side and our two hosts on the other, and shouted across at each other, through the storm of noise, like engineers observing the behaviour of jet engines on a test-bed. My ears still boomed and popped. Dishes appeared on the table at long intervals and in what seemed an arbitrary sequence; a dish of cucumbers, some butter, a cruet. Our male friend, whose name turned out to be Medvedev, asked if we would like some vodka. We said we would. It was produced; I drank some and wondered idly why it seemed to have no effect on me. Then Medvedev drank his and discovered that it was not vodka at all, but white wine. A long argument with the waiter ensued.

The band blasted its way through the same repertory that similar bands were playing in London and Paris. I was introduced to a smiling Indian gentleman, Mr Lal, who had been at Balliol with David Astor. Mr Medvedev made a speech, in which he recommended us to spurn diplomacy and deal frankly with everyone we met. I responded with a short speech of agreement. He then told us a story about a recent visitor from the West who had stayed at this very hotel. After giving up his passport, as required by the regulations, this man had never ventured out of the building, thinking that he would be arrested if he were found walking about with no identifying document. After we had savoured this joke, and drunk some vodka and beer and wine, and eaten caviar and cucumbers, dawn was beginning to streak the sky, my expression of amiability had frozen into a mechanical rictus, and it was decided that we should adjourn for some sleep. After a final exchange of courtesies bawled over the noise of the band, who seemed roused to pandemonium by the sight of our exit, we slumped into the lift and were carried up to the ambassadorial suite, there to dive into merciful oblivion until the insistent shrilling of the telephone, some four hours later, brought me cursing and groping into the daylight.

Owing to the size of the suite, the telephone was thirty or forty yards from the bed, with the result that it stopped ringing just as my hand was about to close on it. I went back to bed and lay staring at the morning sky, already hot and blue with the strong sunlight of a Moscow summer. My sense of unreality had gone. This was the Soviet Union, not the world of the nineteenth-century Russian writers but the heavily-organized, dogma-fed Russia of the present day, and we had committed ourselves to coping with it for a solid month.

First, however, came the question of money. This was owing to me from two sources; the magazine *Novy Mir*, and the Foreign Literature Publishing House. Under the guidance of Lydia, the plump little woman whose acquaintance we had made last night, and who (it slowly transpired) had been assigned by the Writers' Union to accompany us as interpreter and guide, we set off to visit the Editorial Board of the publishing house.

I shall, I think, always remember this visit. To begin with, it set the pattern for all the numerous visits to magazines and publishing houses that we were to make during that month. We entered; the various members of the staff were summoned from their different offices; hands were shaken; then the whole party sat down at a green-baize-covered table on which were cakes, biscuits and glasses of tea, and a question-and-answer session began. It was all very rapid-fire; generally at least half of those present were fluent speakers of English, who would begin by translating everything for the benefit of the others; but once the pace warmed up, there was no longer time to pause between sentences, and my remarks would be translated in an undertone by one person while someone put the next question to me, so that the whole room buzzed with simultaneous conversations. These sessions were interesting, up to a point, but very tiring; after three or four in a day I would be exhausted, and found myself increasingly obliged to duck and side-step the theatre-and-ballet marathon that was supposed to take up our evenings.

This first one differed from the subsequent ones in that we had not merely to establish professional relations but to talk business. I had naturally been asking about the possibility of taking some of my rubles back to England; nobody had seemed able to give me a straight answer, but it appeared that the director of the Foreign Literature Publishing House was in a position, if he chose, to recommend to the financial authorities that I might be allowed to take part of the money, at any rate, in pounds. Lydia told me this in the taxi on our way there, and added that the director was well known for his benevolence, being known to everyone as 'Uncle Paul'. The prospect of being allowed to take home a little of my own money, to solve some of my urgent financial problems at home, began to look a little brighter.

We arrived at the office, which was in one of those curiously rural districts which seem to abound in Moscow. (In fact, I would say that the most attractive feature of Moscow, apart from the exotic jewel of the Kremlin, is this feeling of *rus in urbe*. One finds whole quarters of wooden houses, with overgrown gardens and quiet, tree-lined streets, which seem to belong to some nineteenth-century village. Of course these quarters are scheduled for demolition. The official mind has evidently the same spite against anything with a flavour of the past that one finds in England or America. (Unless it is something that can be turned into a museum piece, and exhibited for a fee, it must be torn down or ruined by a 'development'.) When we had climbed the homely wooden staircase to the magazine's office, Uncle Paul received us, the other members came in one by one, the glasses of tea were produced, and the conference started.

After a few questions and answers of the preliminary nose-rubbing type, during which I was asked if I knew an English writer named James Aldridge (I didn't, at that time), we gradually modulated into discussion of business. Uncle Paul, radiating benevolence, announced that they had been consulting among themselves about the question of my royalties. The sum they were holding for me was evidently a considerable one, and it had been necessary to decide how much should be paid in rubles and how much in pounds.

'So we decided,' he said, beaming at me with an uncle's good-nature, 'to make your money available—'

My face assumed a smile of comradely gratitude.

'—entirely in rubles,' he finished, nodding and smiling grandly.

The smile stayed on my face, but I had the feeling that it had slipped a little to one side.

'We understand how things are with you,' Uncle Paul went on. 'We know you need money in the Soviet Union.'

'I need money at home, too,' I managed to croak.

He nodded. 'So you will be able to have a good trip,' he said. 'Enjoy yourselves! You won't be short of money.'

The other members of the editorial board smiled at me amiably, like so many planets reflecting the life-giving warmth of Uncle Paul. I opened my mouth to protest, but it was no use. Uncle Paul was speaking through an interpreter, which is the perfect not-listening device; I knew that anything I might say would lose all freshness and impact by the time it had been translated; in fact, my remark about needing money at home had not been translated at all.

After this, we knew at least where we stood. The money was to be spent here, or forfeited. We accordingly decided to live it up regardless of expense (no very difficult matter, since we were already inhabiting the ambassadorial suite and paying the equivalent of £3 a head for meals in the hotel restaurant). We would travel : the Black Sea Coast was said to be delightful, and we felt in need of a holiday. Lydia, no doubt relieved at finding that we were not going to drag her on a tour of collectivized cement factories, became all energy and efficiency; plane tickets, boat tickets, cabins, hotel reservations, everything appeared by magic, and after a few more prostrating days in Moscow, we climbed into a sleek jet airliner and flew down to the Black Sea.

The change of scene came none too soon for me. I was beginning to take such a dislike to Moscow that it had become difficult for me to make a fair judgment on it. The all-pervading drabness and dreariness, the joyless crowds shuffling along the streets, the rows of hideous blocks of flats, had begun to settle down on my spirits with a ponderous weight. The gruelling hours spent in question-and-answer sessions round those green-baize tables, the eternity one had to wait to be served with a meal, the slowness and cumbrousness of Rusisan life generally, and—above all—the feeling of endless supervision from above, all combined to produce a melancholia which I could never wholly shake off. Even the little excursions we planned, trying to escape from the present into the past, never quite worked out as they should. We went, naturally, to the Kremlin on our first free afternoon. But it was impossible to surrender ourselves to the fantastic gloomy majesty of those buildings, because we were escorted by two girls, students from Moscow University, who (through no fault of their own) were children of the new age, hostile and rather frightened when confronted with the unusable, immovable bulk of their country's history. One of them, I remember, shrank away with a quite physical movement of disgust on entering the Cathedral and being suddenly confronted with that barbaric, penitential splendour. 'It is a different world . . . I don't like it,' she said to me.

I forebore to remind her that the endless bragging about Sputnik, in which she indulged as much as everyone else, was supposed to be because of the possibility it offered of exploring 'different worlds'. Such a reminder would have been unfair, since the past is one world that must always be closed to people in a revolutionary society. Another time, I asked if we might be shown round Moscow University; I had seen it, there in the centre of the city, and it looked a pleasant eighteenth-century building; I knew that Pushkin had been a student there, and I promised myself an agreeable morning. The girls, all innocently, assumed that I meant the new University, out on the edge of the city, and it was not until we were all in the bus, moving unmistakably away from the centre, that I realized what was happening. Protests were too late; nobody went to the 'old' University; it was only left standing for the time being, till every student and every professor could enjoy the supreme felicity of being housed in a building like the new one.

So to the new University, with great pride, we were taken. It is like a State glue factory.

And indeed, what is manufactured here *is* glue; intellectual and spiritual mucilage. Since students come here from all over the Soviet Union, and none of them are allowed to live in the town, they are all concentrated in this hideous hive stuck up on its hill. For four years or so, these future managers, technicians, party bosses, rulers-and-governors generally, see little of the ordinary citizen whose fate they will decide. It must be in places like this that the seeds of arrogance are sown, that appalling arrogance of the Communist hierarchy against which the younger Russian writers are once more, as I write this, making their noble protest.

Episode at the trial of the poet Brodsky for being socially irresponsible and a parasite:

JUDGE: Who gave you a place among the poets?

BRODSKY: Who gave me a place among the human race?

Of course the same thing happens on the vast campus of an American university—at Berkeley, say. The result, in their case, is a mass of sheer, unsurmountable silliness. Thousands of young people, thrown together month after month, learn to see themselves as an isolated force rather than a living and working part of a social mass that includes old people, children, the middle-aged. They become infected with a hysterical conviction that, since there are so many of them and they are so full of raw energy, they must *do* something. Hence their outbreaks of idiocy, the Dirty Speech Campaign and so forth. This is bad enough. Is the Soviet version, of self-righteousness and lack of imagination, any worse? Time, I suppose, will show.

To get back to my memories. Our trip to the South came just in time; I was beginning to have a grudge against Moscow for a lot of things that were not Moscow's fault. In particular, I was tired of that most exhausting of all pursuits, 'meeting people'. I was tired of the predictability of the conversations. Everybody seemed to lead off with the same two questions. First, did I know James Aldridge? I had to admit that I didn't. Then; what did I think of *Oodva*? *Oodva*, of course, was U2. This American observation plane, flying very high over Soviet territory and loaded with observing and recording equipment of all kinds, had been shot down and its wreckage was on show in a Moscow park where a long queue of people permanently shuffled towards it, to gaze at the sensation of the summer and the final proof of the wickedness of the capitalist warmongers.

I was, in those days, very simple-minded about international politics, espionage, and all the rest of it, but even I knew that the coastlines of Europe and North America are constantly patrolled by Soviet intelligence ships loaded with the same kind of equipment and referred to by both sides as 'trawlers', though it is a long time since anyone mistook them for trawlers. With this kind of thought in my mind, I tried to make light of *Oodva*, but everyone looked accusingly on such levity. Khrushchev himself chose to make a great deal of capital out of it, cancelling a Summit conference that was to have taken place that summer, and generally milking the episode for all the self-righteousness it would yield.

At a Press conference for foreign journalists, Khrushchev launched his familiar tirade about *Oodva*. One of the journalists asked him, 'But surely, Mr Khrushchev, all nations go in for this kind of thing merely as routine?' Khrushchev lost his temper completely. 'I swear to God,' he cried, 'that the Soviet Union has no espionage system. Only capitalist nations do these things.'

Seven short years later there is a change of line, and in the wake of the Philby affair it has become Soviet policy to praise the achievements of their secret service. Russian spying is the best in the world, and has been ever since the Revolution. But meanwhile, we are back in the summer of 1960, the Muscovites are standing patiently in line to see the burnt-out *Oodva*, whose pilot they have imprisoned, and I am being asked forty times a day what I think of it all.

I don't want to think of it at all. I want to sit in the sun, smell Southern flowers, and bathe in the cool, non-political foam.

Oddly enough, one of the things that completed my disillusion with Moscow was a visit to the Zoo. A visit to any Zoo is, of course, a mixed experience; one rarely comes away feeling quite happy about the whole idea of keeping animals in captivity; but if one finds animals fascinating, as I do, it is hard to keep away from them altogether, and I had got the impression from somewhere that Moscow Zoo was a particularly fine one. In this, I was mistaken : it is, or was then, scruffy, ill-stocked, the animals few and in poor condition.

Everything went wrong with this excursion. It was a sticky, head-achy day, with a merciless sun that beat down on the overcrowded asphalt paths. My wife was feeling ill; Lydia, who suffered from fat on the heart, looked suffused and seemed ready to fall down in a fit at any moment; I was thirsty, tired, and oppressed by a feeling of guilt at having suggested the expedition. Still, we were there, so we decided to trudge round. At once, as soon as we saw the first cages, I knew we should not have come. The enclosures were too small; they were unimaginative; and, what was far worse, they were planned in a way that showed no understanding of the needs of the animals. A family of wild pigs, for instance, were in a wire-netting enclosure with a concrete floor. Pigs, as the least zoologically informed person knows, are miserable if they are not allowed to root in the earth; to keep wild pigs permanently on a concrete floor is like putting a bird in a cage where it cannot open its wings. More and more depressed, we moved on past the succession of cramped, unsuitable cages and enclosures. The bears had nothing to clamber on; the wild dogs were in miserable hutches; there was an enclosure of magnificent eagles, hobbling about, their wings clipped to prevent them from flying. This last was a heart-breaking sight; one knew that no one with any feeling for the beauty and majesty of an eagle could possibly subject it to this humiliation. Round and round the great birds walked, clumsily, earthbound with the open sky above their heads. I moved on, quickly. But the next thing I saw was even worse.

Solitary, obviously lost in a misery and loneliness beyond description, stood an old bull elephant. With one foreleg raised an inch or two off the ground, he swayed his great body from side to side, with a rocking, monotonous motion eloquent of sadness and weariness, like a silent form of keening. I asked Lydia if he had ever had a mate. Indeed he had, she answered. There used to be a cow elephant and a calf. What had happened to them? Well, it was all very unfortunate. The calf, when still very tiny, had developed some kind of illness, and they separated it from its mother to allow the veterinary surgeon to attend to it. Unfortunately, they did not take it far enough—only to the other side of the railings. The calf had naturally whimpered under the treatment, and the mother, a few yards away, had tried so hard to get at it and protect it that she had pushed her forehead against the heavy railings, pushed and pushed with all the desperation of frustrated maternal love, until her skull had given away and she had died. The calf, too, had died, and now the old bull stood there, sunk in his grief and solitude, swaying his body to and fro in the sunshine.

After that, I wanted to see no more of the Zoo. I wanted to get away, quickly. I can only stand zoos if they are run by people with some idea of how to look after animals. And in this respect, the Russians are still barbarians. Their idea of looking after animals is about on a level with Western ideas two centuries ago.

I wanted to go, but Lydia had one more thing to show us. We must not, on any account, leave the Zoo without seeing the 'friendship cage'. What was the friendship cage? Ah, we must come and see. It was a typically Soviet idea—a cage in which animals naturally hostile were allowed to grow up together from cubhood, eating out of the same dishes, learning to live together, and generally proving that Mr Khrushchev was right about the possibility of co-existence.

We went over to the Friendship Cage. And suddenly I wanted to burst out crying, from sheer depression. There, in a scruffy, dirty sandpit, sat two dejected bear cubs. On the other side, asleep, was a mangy dog about the size of a collie.

We came to a halt in front of this impressive spectacle. Lydia gazed at it proudly. 'See how the children love it!' she said. And it was true that the sandpit was lined with children, staring. But what they found worth staring at I could not think then and I cannot think now.

But I am not in Moscow to idle about staring at animals; I am a writer, visiting the country of Tolstoy and Dostoievsky, Turgenev and Chekhov. I had hoped to meet some Russian colleagues, but what I actually meet is a number of officials of the Writers' Union. The explanation given is that, since it is summer time, most of the writers are out of town.

But the officials—oh, yes, they are there, summer and winter. Alexei Surkov comes bustling in, beaming, his rimless spectacles flashing in the morning sunlight. He is one of those chunky, square-cut, indestructible middle-aged Russians who are apt to make any Western visitor feel puny and washed-out. He has charm: one feels oneself caught up in it.

As soon as we settle down to talk, Surkov launches, through his interpreter, into a speech about Boris Pasternak, who has just died. 'Poor Boris. He got it all wrong. He should have shared in this experience with us, the great give-and-take of building a new society, instead of going off by himself into a corner and turning his back on it all. An interior emigré—a sad case. And so gifted, so uniquely gifted.'

This speech has the air of having been made a number of times already. I receive it without dissent; Pasternak is, as yet, no more than a name to me. Later, I shall study his work, and come to have some idea of his titanic sufferings and his courage. I shall learn, also, how Surkov, always consumed with a mediocrity's envy, has led the hue and cry against Pasternak from start to finish.

Meanwhile, the sun is still shining, and Surkov knows how to order a lunch. We eat well, drink well, and tell each other, not once but several times, how much we hope for a better understanding between East and West. Surkov's spectacles flash more energetically than ever. He tells a good, though horrifying, story about an experience of his during the war, when a Russian and a German airman fought an aerial battle just overhead. The Russian's plane caught fire, and he jumped out, with no parachute, and landed at Surkov's feet. 'His bones cracked like firewood,' says Surkov.

Back at the hotel, we compare impressions. My wife, who is very responsive to everything Russian, is ready to like Surkov. I am not quite so ready; not because I am more perceptive than she is, but because I have an ingrained distrust of literary people who get themselves into official positions.

Two vignettes from the south.

We are in Yalta. It is a hot evening; the air is laden with heavy, spicy fragrance. We are walking, my wife and I, along some sort of footway; in a public garden, perhaps. (For Yalta, which grew up as a holiday and health resort for metropolitan Russia after the development of the railway, is full of these pleasaunces.) Having nowhere to go, being out of doors merely for its own sake, we sit down on a stone bench. The pathway is crowded, but presently a figure threads its way towards our bench and sits down beside us. He is an old man, tall and stooped; he wears a white linen suit such as one might wear in the tropics, and in one tired old hand he carries a string bag full of what appear to be mineral water bottles. But he has not given up; his white beard is neatly clipped to a point.

We both look at him with intense, covert interest. Our heads are full of Chekhov, since this very day we have been at Chekhov's house, and this man beside us is old enough to have been a boy at school during the years of Chekhov's greatest triumphs, when the Moscow Arts Theatre company came down to Yalta, and acted his plays for him because he was too ill to go to them. Nor is it a matter of age only. He looks like a Chekhov character; or, rather, since Chekhov wrote about every possible kind of Russian character and his complete works form a definitive Russian *Comédie Humaine*, I had better say that he looks like what Western theatre-goers are in the habit of thinking of as a Chekhov character; a member of the slightly seedy gentry or the *intelligentsia.*

His head is sunk on his chest. God knows what thoughts are going through his mind as he sits there in his old linen suit. Presently, gathering up his string bag with a clanking of bottles, he rises and moves slowly away. From first to last he has shown no awareness that there is anyone else on the bench. Probably, if he had known that two visitors from the West, emissaries from the world outside the fortress in which he has lived since 1917, were sitting close to him, he still would not have glanced at us. It is too late, his life is too nearly over; he is like Firs, forgotten in the empty house.

The second vignette. We are in a hired car, with Lydia, going from Sochi to Ritza. Sochi is a fashionable holiday town, and Lydia has been looking forward to a few days there. But, after a day or two, we have become restless there. (It is a kind of Crimean Bournemouth.) Hungry for the wilderness, we have asked to be taken to Lake Ritza, up in the Caucasus, which we have heard, somehow or other, is a place that can be visited for holidays. Lydia is disappointed, but she makes the arrangements, and we set off.

The car is a Ziss or a Zim or whatever they call that heavy, badly designed car that seems to be always driven by a chauffeur and carries important comrades from place to place. The chauffeur is a brute. He keeps his foot remorselessly on the accelerator so that we are thrown from side to side and bounced up and down. We appeal to him, through Lydia, to go more slowly; his response is to give a brief, sardonic grin, ease off for perhaps five seconds, and then drive on as fast as ever. The road is as twisting as a corkscrew; the occasional straight stretches are no help, because as soon as the driver can see a hundred yards ahead he immediately accelerates up to eighty miles an hour. Once, he slams over a particularly bad bump at this speed, and we both fly up and bang our heads on the ceiling. Lydia is sitting in front; it is not quite so bad for her, and in any case she is talking without a pause and notices nothing else; the beautiful, hypnotic Russian language has her in thrall. But we are suffering. My wife is pregnant, she is feeling far from well, and it is torment to her to be rolled from side to side and flung up and down. We try and try to appeal to the brute of a driver, but he is determined to go at his own speed, which is nothing short of flat out. If I had a revolver I would gladly shoot him.

Suddenly, roaring round a tight bend with the tyres sobbing and the horrible car careering on to its horrible side, we slam on all brakes and rock to a halt. There, in front of us, blocking the road, is a herd of cattle.

Delighted, we settle back on the seat and look forward to the blessed respite of travelling at five miles an hour, if only for a moment. But there is even better to come. In charge of the herd —I now see, to my joy—are three wonderful ruffians on horseback. I have never seen more wonderfully *insouciant* men. One, evidently their president, carries a long rifle and sports a magnificent head of curly hair coming half-way down his back. He wears long boots of soft leather, and grins insolently at the driver. I wish I knew whatever language it is he speaks, so that I could wind the window down and tell him how much I like and admire him.

The driver, scowling, puts his head out and snarls what is evidently the equivalent of 'Get those things out of the way'. The trio grin at him joyously, and their leader makes what is clearly a satirical reply. My wife and I hug each other for sheer elation. The driver begins sullenly to jab at his horn. He goes on sounding it, with absolutely no effect, for at least a quarter of an hour, until he is finally able to nudge his way through the massed rumps of the animals.

Lydia turns in her seat and gives us a rather embarrassed smile. This kind of thing, she says, is apt to happen when you are dealing with Georgians. 'They do not like us Russians,' she says. I like her for admitting this so frankly, for of course the official line is that all the other republics look to Moscow through a tearful mist of love and gratitude.

Stalin, being a Georgian, saw to it that the régime lay less heavily on Georgia than on the rest of the country. I already knew that as a textbook fact; but, since catching a glimpse of those three wonderful *mauvais sujets*, I know what it really means.

Lydia was very human. She was perfectly willing to admit that people are normally fallible, even in the Soviet Union, and this made her a good filter against the self-righteousness that is so all-pervading and so trying. She alone, of all the people we met in such numbers, was willing to tell us of mistakes and failures. It preserved a tiny drop of sanity in the Alice-in-Wonderland world of Soviet officialdom.

At the same time, of course, she was a loyal Communist patriot. This had the interesting result of giving her, at times, a complete mental block against English. If I asked a question that could not be answered without admitting some contradiction in the system, she usually either failed to hear me or misunderstood my meaning. Her stock answer at these times was 'Yes, of course', always delivered with a vague, tired smile.

She was a nice woman. When we parted from her, she shed tears, though we had been difficult and demanding and she might well have been glad to see the back of us. But she was the kind of person who naturally weeps at parting from anyone; forming attachments easily, she broke them with difficulty.

How human and tender-hearted Lydia was we did not fully appreciate until, in the last ten days of our stay, we were given a new interpreter. This was a younger woman, by name Oksana. Where Lydia was of an age to have received her upbringing before Communist attitudes became all-powerful, Oksana was a true product of the régime; a revolutionary fanatic to the last flash of the eyes and tightening of the lips. Her guard was never down. She would never, for instance, have told us about the death of the baby elephant in the Zoo. She would have been more likely to say that the animal was killed by a poison bun given to it by a capitalist visitor, maddened with jealousy because his own country had no zoos. And if we had tried to tell her that capitalist countries do have zoos, she would not have heard us, because she was supremely skilled in the art of not listening.

Her technique, in this respect, was quite different from Lydia's. The loyalty which made Lydia unwilling to see defects in the Soviet system occasionally came into conflict with the gentleness and courtesy which made her unwilling to quarrel or contradict. Hence the refuge in vagueness, the tired smile and the 'Yes, of course'. Oksana was altogether different. There was nothing 'psychological', as people say, about *her* not-listening. She didn't listen because she damned well wasn't going to listen. If you said anything that tended either to the credit of the Western nations or to criticism of the Soviet Union, she simply cut you short in mid-sentence.

It had originally been the intention of the Writers' Union to assign Oksana to us as our interpreter during the whole month of our stay, but since Russian arrangements never work quite perfectly, she had at the last minute been assigned to Sir Charles and Lady Snow (a fact which, for one reason or another, often comes back to my mind) and was now free to come to us because they had gone home. I shall, I think, always be grateful for the kind fate that sent us three weeks of Lydia. I could never have stood a month of Oksana's relentless brain-washing, and might have been driven by it to some mad act of rebellion, an international scandal.

To some people this will sound excessive; but I shall be believed by anyone who has travelled in Russia and knows the atmosphere of constant frustration, the endless changing of arrangements, the impenetrable mystery that surrounds every simple procedure, the colossal struggle that is involved in getting hold of trivial necessities such as a needle and thread or a packet of envelopes. One is constantly driven out of patience. And all this to the accompaniment of ceaseless boasting about the régime, and an utter refusal to hear anything in favour of *our* way of doing things.

An example. I wish to go to the cinema. Naturally, I would rather see good films than bad, but if no specially good films are showing I will settle for whatever happens to be on; it will be interesting to see what kind of run-of-the-mill films the Soviet industry turns out. In Moscow, Lydia undertakes to get us to a film, but unspecified difficulties arise; the film is not on after all, or tickets are not to be had; I do not understand how difficult is the thing I am demanding.

So, in Sochi, we try again. Lydia knows of a cinema; we will go, that very evening. After dinner, we set off, but when we get to the cinema we find that the programme has been cancelled and the cinema is being used for a political meeting. No matter; there is another cinema in town, and this one *is* showing a film. We get on to the bus, to go there, and I am so buoyed up by the thought of an evening's carefree entertainment that, as I hang on to the strap, I unguardedly allow myself to whistle like a schoolboy. My whistling is not very loud, but it seems to the conductress a breach of decorum, not to be permitted on her bus, and she snaps at me. I insist on having her words translated, and they turn out to be, 'Stop that whistling: this is a public place'.

After that, I do not whistle. We get to the cinema without further incident and sit through the film, a piece of patriotic flummery about the gallant Russian resistance, in 1939, against the terrible Finns. Later, back in Moscow once more, we succeed in getting to a cinema again, and this time it is a patriotic film about the war against the Germans. I begin to wonder whether the Russian film industry turns out anything except patriotic films. But then Oksana tells me (for by this time, we are under her guidance) that there is a chance to see a film of Gogol's *Dead Souls.* I jump at this, as one last chance to see a Soviet film of serious quality while I am here. But soon the inevitable difficulties begin. No one seems to know what time the film is being shown. 'We will find out tomorrow.' When tomorrow comes, we are told that the showing is at 2 p.m. Since we are not due to lunch till 1.15, and therefore have no reasonable chance of getting up from the table before 4.00, I dismiss the matter from my mind. Later in the day, I am casually told, in the middle of a discussion on something else, that the film starts at four o'clock. I ask if we can go, the next day, at this time. Certainly! But—another fact casually introduced—this version of *Dead Souls* is not a film in the true sense, but a stage production that has been filmed in order to bring it to a wider public. Since this robs it of any cinematic interest, I once again dismiss the matter from my mind. The final stage comes when, twenty-four hours before our ship is to sail, I am told (i) that the film is not a stage production after all, but a genuine piece of cinema, and (ii) that there is a showing on the following day at eleven in the morning. Do we want to go? We do not. It is our last morning, and we have arranged to do all our shopping.

In the event, another English visitor, who has come ashore from a cruise ship (we are now in Leningrad), takes the ticket and goes to see the film. Oksana later tells me, with a forbearing smile, that this gentleman has 'enjoyed the film very much'. Her expression conveys that I, after putting everyone to endless trouble, suddenly and unaccountably washed my hands of the whole affair, leaving the situation to be saved by our kindly fellow-countryman.

This fellow-Englishman, as it happens, is a writer. He has come to Leningrad on a cruise, and is living on the ship and coming ashore for a few hours each day. He has not even the experience of Russian life that could be gained from staying in a Russian hotel, whereas we have travelled thousands of miles and stayed at every kind of place. This does not, however, inhibit him from giving us his views on Soviet life and institutions, and even, with kindly laughter, correcting our errors.

'I'm going to see Professor Dacha this afternoon,' he tells me with innocent pride. I can only conclude that he means he is to be taken into the country, to the *dacha* of some Professor. It occurs to me to hope that his grip on Russian life and customs will have improved by the time he gets home and is accepted as an authority.

In the event, this hope is disappointed.

It is a summer morning in Leningrad, with a balmy air blowing in from the sea. Oksana and my wife are off somewhere, and I am alone for the first time since coming to Russia nearly a month ago, walking without care in a public garden.

A young man looks up at me from a bench as I go by. His glance attracts mine, and I see that he is reading an English paperback book, a Pelican on some historical subject. This marks him out as having some contact with visitors, for he could not have bought this book at a Soviet bookshop. He sees me looking at it and says, smiling, 'I like to get both sides of these historical questions'.

I sit down beside him and we go into a conversation. Presently he is joined by another young man. They make an interesting contrast; my first interlocutor is tall and slender, thin-faced, a typical intellectual, rather Baltic-looking; the newcomer, his friend, is a chunky youth, with muscles, in a T-shirt. They are both students. The intellectual speaks English perfectly, the tough quite passably.

My wife now joins us, and the boys offer to show us where they live. For a wonder, Oksana is not present, and we seize the opportunity to go, unsupervized, in a non-official *milieu.* They take us to a tall, rather crumbling house, up several flights of stairs and into a small room with two single beds in it and not much else. They show the room because they know we will be interested in seeing it, but they do not pretend to like it. They don't care for life in this house; the neighbours are nosey and complaining.

In a few minutes, we have to hurry away to keep some appointment but later in the day manage to meet the two young men again. Once more I am by myself, but they have two girls with them. One of the girls is nondescript, but the other catches my eye; she is small, blonde, with china-blue eyes, a button nose and very high cheekbones, obviously from some stock of the far north of Europe. Sure enough, they tell me she is Latvian.

This time, we meet in a café, and eat and drink something or other, and the tall young man sits next to me, speaking quietly and urgently. He feels cornered. He is in bad political odour, as a generally *fainéant* type; he used to have a job with Intourist, but he has been dismissed from it and has twice recently been arrested and held for questioning; the second time was very tough. He sees nothing ahead except 'Siberia or worse'. Now comes the explanation of why he got into talk with me in the park this morning. He is desperate to establish contact with any visitor who might help him and his friend to make their escape from Soviet territory. 'Do you think Scotland Yard could get us out?' he asks me. I don't know what to say; obviously he thinks that Scotland Yard is some kind of cloak-and-dagger organization. I try to tell him that Scotland Yard is in any case a purely internal organization to combat British criminals. We leave the matter in the air. He suggests another meeting, on the following evening, and I agree to it. Perhaps, in the meantime, one of us will have an idea. Perhaps.

Now the talk becomes more general. With perfect openness, the tall young man tells me that they are going to take the girls back to their room and spend the night with them on their two little beds. Sex, presumably *à quatre*, is about the only thing the régime has not managed to police out of existence. I don't know whether the girls would blush if they understood English; somehow, I don't imagine so. They must know, anyway, that the boy is telling me what they are going to do. (I now see why the neighbours sometimes complain, just as they would in Birmingham.) The Latvian girl looks strangely like a doll, pretty but full of sawdust. She would be a new-born baby when Stalin grabbed her country and turned it into a province of the Soviet Union. Or perhaps, if she is under twenty, not yet born. At any rate, she will have no memories of living in a country where people had freedom and could choose their own way of life. So, like the other young people here, she is taking the only line left open to her that seems to lead to any kind of fulfilment.

Perhaps I am putting thoughts into her head that don't belong there. Northern Europeans are strange anyway; their eyes often have that empty look. But she has been robbed, this girl; the flesh and blood have been taken out of her and replaced by sawdust, the dry detritus of Soviet propaganda. Would we react much differently? If England were occupied and swamped by a much larger neighbour, its government annexed, its traditions obliterated, its populace spied on by a secret police, wouldn't some at least of the girls become like this one, poor lost little amateur whores, getting what fun they could from sexual monkey-tricks in a shabby room?

I like her better than Oksana, anyway. And I like the Baltic-looking young man better than Surkov. I suppose this makes me a hopeless case.

We say goodbye on the pavement, reiterating that we will meet in the park on the following evening at nine o'clock. I give the Latvian girl a sudden, impulsive peck on the cheek. Everybody laughs. Afterwards, I can't decide what made me want to kiss her. I think I was trying to tell her something, but what?

The next day, it is our turn to 'go to see Professor Dacha'. Oksana tells us that a visit has been arranged for us, to the *dacha* of a professor of English literature. We drive out there in the early afternoon, and before we set out I establish carefully that we shall be back well before nine o'clock.

The professor's *dacha* is in a beautiful area of pine forest, near the sea. It would seem to me even more beautiful if I had not been told, very proudly, that the whole area has been set aside for these summer residences of scholars and literary men. That one fact seems to put me back in the Zoo, with the lonely old bull elephant. Still, no doubt it is convenient. The intelligentsia can continue their discussions as they stroll in the forest or on the sea-shore. And that is just what we did do, in between eating and drinking at the *dacha*. The professor is a harmless old man, well broken in. He has taught English all through the Stalin era, when any kind of contact with England was strictly forbidden, and his life's work has consisted of putting English literature through the meat-grinder of Soviet theory. He tells me, in rather halting English, that he once published an article on Sir Thomas More, and takes down the periodical in which the article was printed, and shows me the yellowing pages with a touching pride. His eyes glow gently as he recalls that he once made a visit to Paris; in 1910, it was. Paris in 1910, the Paris of Apollinaire, of Picasso, of Satie, of Marcel Schwob, of Arnold Bennett, seems remote enough to me; what it must be like to him, after those long years in the Zoo, I daren't think. He is a gentle soul. With him at the *dacha* is his daughter, a handsome, clear-eyed girl. She speaks much better English than her father, being the product of more up-to-date teaching methods. At one point the daughter happens to mention her age, which is about ten years more than one would guess from her appearance, and Oksana cannot repress a start of surprise. 'I am well preserved,' says the young woman, quietly. It is exactly the same idiom as an Englishwoman of the same type would use.

Meanwhile, time is getting on. We are about ninety minutes' drive from Leningrad, and I still have my eye on that nine o'clock appointment. Six o'clock, seven o'clock, come and go. I begin to remind Oksana. 'Yes, we will go,' she says soothingly. Half-past seven, eight, half-past eight : 'Yes, we will go.' At last it dawns on me, innocent and ignorant fool, that she has never, from the beginning, had the slightest intention of getting me back by nine o'clock. Perhaps I have been watched and my movements reported on; in any case, the mere fact that I had made an independent arrangement, and proposed to go off hob-nobbing with persons unknown, would be enough to settle the matter.

As we roll into Leningrad at well past eleven (Oksana is taking no chances), I try a feeble remonstrance. She smiles soothingly. 'Yes, but it was so interesting, talking to the professor. I would not have felt justified in cutting it short.' 'But I had a definite appointment to see some people.' She shrugs, calmly. 'They will understand.'

Understand what? That they don't matter? That they mustn't start having a social life with Western visitors?

Once again, the end has justified the means.

Those two boys, obviously, are to be counted among the failures of the system. And the professor, with his gentle, broken smile, does not strike me as a man who has found much to rejoice at in his life. His daughter, for all her quiet dignity, has something of the spinster's underlying sadness when she tells us that she is well preserved.

I cannot shake off the feeling that I have been moving among characters from Chekhov. I recall that the critic Merezhkovski, who must have been the sort of fool that is bred in academies of criticism, accused Chekhov of writing too much about 'failures'. Chekhov's own point of view on this matter is well known. 'One would need to be a God,' he said, 'to decide which are the failures and which are the successes in this life.'

When I think back to the two boys, the one with his T-shirt and muscles and the other with his long, intellectual, Baltic face, to the old Professor showing me his article on Thomas More, to his daughter with her youthful appearance and her air of loneliness, to the china-doll eyes of the Latvian girl, and then to Surkov with his false, bouncing geniality and Oksana with her gimlet smile, this sentence of Chekhov's comes again and again to my mind.

This sharpened sense of what Chekhov and other major Russian writers start from, the kind of people they write about, is the chief benefit I got from my visit to the country.

The Russia of Turgenev, the Russia of Chekhov, the Russia of Pasternak.

A Russian friend, an émigré in his sixties, is sitting by our fireside, telling us a story of those wild days in 1919. He is a tall, dignified man, grey-haired; a man of solid learning, who speaks in a slow, emphatic voice; but always, behind his glasses, lurks that flashing Russian humour, so unlike English jocularity or facetiousness.

'We are in White territory, in Kiev.' (I shall always hear his voice, giving a wonderfully whole-hearted Russian diphthong to *Kiev.*) 'All the time, we can hear gun-fire. We children cannot get on with our lessons. So our father, who is a Professor at the university, decides to take us away to the south, to be further from the Bolsheviks. We lock up the house, leave a note explaining what we have done, and set off for the railway station with what belongings we can carry. With us is another Professor who has two small children. One of them, he carries on his neck'—here my friend bends his head forward and gives himself a vigorous smack on the back of the neck—'and the other, my father carried, on *his* neck.' I can see those two burdened, scholarly necks, moving towards the railway station. 'We also have with us the Assistant Professor of Astronomy, a young man. At the station, everything is cha-a-os. After some hours, a train comes in and we squeeze on to it. The train moves on for half an hour and then it stops and we are thrown off again. We get on again. This goes on for many hours. Finally, about half-way through the following day, we get to a town, we do not know what kind of town, but we decide that it will do and we will stop here. We get off the train. The professor with the small children goes on; he is going right down to the South. But we still have with us the Assistant Professor.

'The station master has a large urn of hot water, which he gives to anyone wishing to make tea. We have a samovar but we have no tea. People are there who have just arrived from the South, and they give us tea and other supplies.

'We walk out of the station into the centre of the town. The centre of the town is a marsh. We ask if there is an hotel. "No," an immense shrug, "there is no hotel". Is there anywhere we can stay? "Well," another shrug, "you can go to the monastery". The monastery is outside the town. We set off, carrying our belongings. We leave the town and are going over the fields, and we meet a man in military uniform. "Where are you going?" "To the monastery." "But what do you want at the monastery?" "Somewhere to stay."' A wave of the hand. ' "You need not go to the monastery. There is room to stay at my house." So we set off for the officer's house.

'He explains on the way that the house has been looted, four or five times in the last six months, and there is nothing much there. But the beds are there. The bedsteads, even some of the mattresses. We arrive there, and we see for ourselves. It is enough. We can sleep here. In one room, on the only complete bed, is lying a beautiful young woman. She has tuberculosis of the hip. She must lie still for many months, and have—good—food.' (These last words with special emphasis. No doubt the implication is that the beautiful girl must die, since there is no good food to be had.)

'We move in. My parents take over the running of the household. They do the shopping, the planning, the cooking—everything. Meanwhile the officer, who is an artillery officer and acquainted with mathematics, begins a discussion with the Assistant Professor of Astronomy. The officer has been playing patience, and the question is whether the game of patience can be translated into mathematical equations. All day they argue. Each day they take the matter up again. They lay out the cards, they cover sheets of paper with figures.'

Is this not exactly the world of *Dr Zhivago*? The officer and the young professor arguing about mathematics in the looted house, while the beautiful young girl lies dying, the refugee scholar and his wife scour the district for food, and the uprooted, dazed child who will one day become an historian watches and remembers: it could be a scene invented by a great novelist.

But only by a great *Russian* novelist.

So, having started in literature, I finish in literature, and Russia is once more to me what it was for so many years: a place of the mind. Despotism flourishes there; very well, let it flourish. By a fantastic historical coincidence, the particular despotism that was ushered in by the events of 1917 got itself mixed up with the noble and generous dream of freedom and equality which had haunted the mind of Europe since the eighteenth century, and to which some gave the name of socialism. Very well, let it be entwined. The contemporary phase of Russian despotism will have its paid agents and its unpaid agents; it will have its propagandists who are salaried in flattery and hospitality. (What Western writer will lunch with Surkov today, I wonder? And who will be taken to see Professor Dacha?) My testimony has been given, to all that; henceforth, I opt out.

I love the Russia I see when I close my eyes, that great ocean of land, where wolves run through the endless forests, where the cart-ruts fill with gleaming water in the spring rain, where people talk hour after hour, with inexhaustible passion, about what is going on in their minds, and drink glasses of tea and talk again, till dawn comes up outside the windows and head-shawled women hurry to obey the church bells; where a gentleman with a long gun, and a game-bag over his shoulder, knocks at a peasant's hut and asks for a night's shelter; where the railway engines are fuelled with birch-logs; where the human spirit, in spite of the malice of unbreakable tyranny, guards its freedom in some inner fastness, so that at any unexpected moment it can happen that we hear a Russian voice saying something swift and leaping and unanswerable. 'Who gave you a place among the poets?' 'Who gave me a place among the human race?'

PART THREE

Epilogue

can override all others—which will, inevitably, happen from time to time—but that it *ought* to do so, that this is a moral imperative.

One tries to be sympathetic; if only because mere indignation, mere uncomprehending opposition, is an empty emotion. Puritanism has, in time, moved mountains. What one fears is that when the mountains have been moved, we are left with a featureless plain that is easily covered over with concrete. The Puritanism that worked within the societies of northern Europe in the sixteenth and seventeenth centuries was motivated by a wish to have done with the Middle Ages and in particular with the multiplicity of religious observances, and the consequent proliferation of religious attitudes, that characterized the Age of Faith. This Puritanism acted as a valuable catalyst on the literary culture of the West inasmuch as it provoked the Renaissance 'Defences of Poetry', which were not, of course, defences of verse-writing but of imaginative writing itself. The conflict sharpened until we find Oliver Cromwell ordering his soldiers to smash the stained glass windows in English churches and knock the heads off statues. Much good art was lost. We, the inheritors, are the poorer for his action. Yet the Puritanism he represented was no merely negative thing. It contributed, and we have what it contributed. The art that Cromwell ordered to be destroyed was associated in the Puritan mind with idolatry, with a plurality of vision that menaced the single eye of Protestant worship; and, politically, with a governing class that was soft on Popery. The Puritan of the 1640s was intent on replacing these things with a marvellously bracing theocentric vision of the universe. He attacked art in the name of something greater: of course the Puritan always does this, but Cromwell's vision of what religion and society might be, his dedication to a City of Man that really might achieve a certain very direct relationship with a City of God, was at any rate something important. In the name of what greater thing do our modern Puritans attack art? For they, make no mistake, would knock the heads off statues if they could. Indeed, the determined effort to substitute Anti-Art for Art, the sustained attempt to interest us in Campbell's soup tins and heaps of gravel tossed on to the studio floor, *is* a way of knocking the heads off statues and throwing acid on paintings, just as the 'sound poem' is an attack on the notion of a poetic language which can compass a wide range of human emotions.

The criteria of the modern Puritan are social. He postulates no City of God overarching his City of Man. He wants, or claims to want, social justice, a world dedicated to the interests of the majority, an end to the plight of the poor. These, by themselves, are noble aims. One's misgivings begin when one contemplates the people who voice these aims. Some of them, indeed, are all that they claim to be. These, the ones who truly mean what they say and are prepared to make sacrifices, usually meddle very little with art. Their lives are filled with a blazing, acrid vision that leaves them in no need of the colour and rhythm and movement that art would offer; while towards the inevitable complication of art, arising from the fact that art mirrors the complication of life, they would feel, if they came face to face with it, only a virtuous horror.

It is the Puritan who does meddle with art, who does try to police it, to forbid it, to channel it into a purpose that suits his emotional needs, who must—to be blunt—be rejected out of hand as a nuisance, a fractious child interfering with grown-up people. He is a simplifier, and art can have no truck with simplification. It cannot simply preach Liberation or Revolution, inasmuch as these are two-dimensional things, belonging to the world of imperatives, and art is rich with the multi-dimensional richness of life. It has a memory, and Revolution has no memory. It includes negatives and counter-stresses, and Liberation cannot afford these. It glows with colour, and Puritanism is black and white like a newspaper headline.

The Puritan attempt to simplify art, so as to muzzle and direct it and also to avoid its challenge, is usually carried out by failed artists who have adopted the Puritan ethos as a cover for their failure. At the level of art-chatter, therefore, Puritanism joins hands with that other arch-simplifier, sensationalism.

Pseudo-art takes many forms. In our time, the pseudo-artist is generally both a Puritan and a sensation-monger. To be sensational is to attract attention, and it is the duty of the

Puritan, the man with a simplifying mission, to attract attention if he can. Hence the cult of the extreme statement. It is as if our age has grown deaf to any language except that of the superlative. Slender talents, competing with one another in staking out the ultimate boundaries of whatever they are trying to express, occupy the forefront of attention. The pornography of sexuality, which has always been with us, is now challenged by the pornography of violence, the pornography of disgust, and the pornography of despair. (It is not at all my purpose, in this essay, to attack individuals, but I should like to take this opportunity of going on record with the opinion that Samuel Beckett, whom I have never met and against whom I feel no personal animus whatsoever, is a writer with a very minor talent and that the present inflation of his reputation will come to seem, in retrospect, one of those interesting collective lapses of taste like the Victorian admiration for Martin Tupper.)

The rise of pornography, of course, has other explanations. It is connected with the Puritan insistence on explicitness. To the Puritan, it is a deadly sin to sweep anything under the carpet. Imagination is suspect because imagination so often works best on what is under the carpet or behind a veil of one kind or another. There must be no carpets, no veils! The Puritan fiercely disapproves, and perhaps rightly, of the merely suggestive; of the kind of play or novel that won a large public by encouraging people to think about sex, without making any explicit sexual statement. And, since it is now considered a moral weakness to shy away from sex and say nothing about it, the Puritan is left with only one alternative: the totally explicit which sometimes passes for 'permissiveness', though there is nothing permissive about it: it is authoritarian, exhortatory, a categorical imperative. Do this, or be damned! Sit in your theatre seat and watch a couple on stage actually having intercourse—because to avert your eyes, or walk out, merely on the grounds that such acts have no proper audience except the people concerned in them, is to reject the explicit statement: and Puritanism lives by the explicit statement, and will accept nothing else. And if it is compulsory to accept copulation on stage, it is necessarily just as compulsory to swallow a book like *Last Exit to Brooklyn* without gagging—even, if one is a determined enough Puritan, to get up in court and testify that it is Literature.

That last thought, of course, brings us into contact with another wing of the present onslaught on imaginative literature. It brings us to the academic, since one of the functions that academic teachers of literature have agreed to take over is that of helping the legal system to decide what is, or is not, an offence against public decency. I suppose the historic date here is the *affaire Lady Chatterley* in 1960 or thereabouts. It was that hearing which first alerted the legal and political mind to the fact that the scholarly-critical mind was, on the whole, in favour of the removal of restraints. Academic here joins with Puritan in the insistence on explicitness and the sin of sweeping anything under the carpet. If it is wrong that a fiercely moral Puritan like D. H. Lawrence should be muzzled, then it quickly becomes wrong that *anyone* should be muzzled.

What I personally miss, in the to-and-fro of this argument, is any concern for the nature of art, the way in which art gets its effects. The assumption all along is that anything that can't be said in so many words can't be said at all. Yet Shakespeare in *Antony and Cleopatra* managed to convey the full range of sexual passion without using a single word that we should recognize as indecent. Sexually, it is probably the most highly charged work in English literature, yet it contains actually less bawdy, less indecency for indecency's sake, than almost any other Shakespearean play. Shakespeare is a great enough artist to work by suggestion. He harnesses the reader's sexual imagination instead of pouring out the untreated contents of his own. In this, he is merely being true to the fundamentals of his art. All art works by suggestion as much as by explicitness, and suggestion is a means of working on the recipient's mind which resembles judo: throw him by his own weight! The modern liberated writer, splattering the page with every four-letter word in the language, actually chills the reader's imagination, producing a sense of weariness and surfeit not only with his own efforts but, what is much more serious, with the natural impulses he is trying to exploit. So that one hears time and time again the complaint from ordinary intelligent readers that this or that sex-obsessed book is 'enough to put me off sex'. This is the result of that denial of imagination which allows the reader no participatory role.

This denial, in turn, comes from the Puritan belief that the imagination is hostile because unbiddable. That belief is very dominant in the world nowadays. All totalitarian régimes hold it as a matter of course (the imagination feeds on freedom, therefore it deserves to starve). But it is also widespread in those societies whose governmental systems disclaim any such total wish to process the individual. (I had almost written 'democracies', but that word must now be deemed obsolete; the technological world has screened out individual freedom and with it the political ideal of interpreting the will of Demos, on any large scale. There can be democracy within the village cricket club, but not at national level—a fact which by itself constitutes the major argument for decentralization.) This distrust of the imagination is a predictable result of the immense speeding-up of the means of communication which has resulted in our present state of perpetual wooziness, that 'information overload' of which we have learnt to speak blandly. When everything that happens everywhere in the world is instantaneously reported, not only does any one separate event become meaningless, we quickly arrive at a state in which *all* events are meaningless, and since that way lies nothing but insanity and disintegration, we strive vainly to subject this torrent of events to a simultaneous, production-line process of interpretation. Naturally this interpretation cannot be pursued rigorously, since there is a long queue of other subjects waiting to be processed, hence the mania for interviewing (a form of exposure which does not really expose anything, the subject of the interview being always a puppet with strings pulled by the hard-faced professional who is working him over) and for the panel discussion (another means of appearing to put a topic into perspective which actually involves it in a hall-of-mirrors of conflicting perspectives, a perfect recipe for the intellectual slapstick which television has taught us to accept instead of thought). In this state of grogginess, a non-stop mainlining on the potent mix peddled by the media in all countries, there is no place for the imagination, if only because the imagination works in depth and at leisure, and the effect of our collective media trip is to seal off the depths of our minds and to deny us any slackening of pace.

This situation is not irremediable. One of the features I like and admire about young people at the present time, those below twenty-five in particular, is their complete and casual rejection of the electronic-and-plastic world their parents rushed forward so eagerly, between 1945 and 1955, to embrace. And, since many of these young people are to be found in the universities, that alone makes the universities so much the more healthy and pleasant to the spirit. As regards their elders, however, the hard-line professional academics, I feel less certain of grounds for optimism. It is disconcerting, for one thing, to note how, with no apparent inner conflict, academics as a whole have accepted the opportunity to 'reach a wider audience' (i.e. travesty their intellectual tradition with maximum publicity and profitableness) by means of the television panel industry. For another, and this particularly concerns those whose stamping-ground is what used to be called 'the humanities', I am disturbed by the symptoms of what I discern as a new academism, as crippling as anything in the old: a refusal to join in the complex, wide-ranging and subtly-tinged interchange between present and past.

Let me explain. I belong to the generation of men of letters formed in the era of T. S. Eliot, and I still accept Eliot as an important authority in matters that concern me professionally. One of Eliot's main preoccupations, as we all know, was the dialogue between past and present. His first really influential utterance, the essay 'Tradition and the Individual Talent' (1919), was to the effect that, while it has long been understood that the past influences the present, it is also true that the present influences the past. If a new artist arises whose work modifies our way of looking at his particular art, we then apply that modified vision to the masterpieces of our tradition, and we may have to do some adjusting of reputations. The backward look alters the object. This view, needless to say, was very unpopular with academics, who live on received judgements and dislike having to make changes, and who also derive income from text-books which they do not wish to see outdated. But Eliot, blandly immovable, persisted in it. He never budged from the position, stated in 'Tradition and the Individual Talent', that the historical sense is 'nearly indispensable to anyone who would continue to be a poet beyond his twenty-fifth year'; nor from his view that the useful critic is the man who is aware of the reach of the past, and who uses this awareness to illuminate the problem of the present.

It has happened to me many times, in the last five or six years, to meet people employed in university literary studies, both research and teaching, who have taken up a quite contrary line. To these people, the present age is so totally new, so totally unlike any former age in human history, that nothing from the past can be carried over. Certain figures who constantly recur in my conversation as measuring-points, people as diverse as Shakespeare and Samuel Johnson and Ovid and Chekhov and Marvell, were waved aside as belonging to that sealed-off, unreachable 'past'. Listening to these opinions, I have been haunted by a sense of having heard them, or something not quite unlike them, in my youth; I have murmured inwardly,

> For [she] is like to something I remember
> A great while since, a long, long time ago.

And now it comes back to me. When I was a young student, the older professors were very firmly of the opinion that there could be no fruitful dialogue between past and present. They wanted the contemporary artist to be the docile servant of his great predecessors. In poetry, for instance, they liked best the kind of gentle, well-smoothed lyrical verse that derived primarily from Tennyson; and if such verse was not quite as important as Tennyson's, who was troubled by that? Innovation, in any of the arts, earned their fierce hostility. The arts were complete; great painters, great composers, great writers, had lived and had shown the way. Where was the sense in trying to meddle with things that were settled and done with?

Not all senior academics took this line; but it can fairly be called the characteristic attitude among them. And when I hear the trendy young academic of today dismiss the past as unreachable, I realize that I am in the presence of a new academism as hidebound as the old. Obviously, the claim that present-day life is unrecognizably different from anything that went before is so much self-important twaddle. The emotional infrastructure of human life is apt to show small but interesting differences from one epoch to another; it was not quite the same in sixteenth-century Europe as in classical antiquity, to say nothing of the racial differences between Africa, the East and the West; but to cut it off with a chopper, to say that since certain technological disorientations the entire nature of the human animal has altered —this is merely another symptom of 'information overload' and the failure of imagination.

After all this, what?

I am trying to resist the temptation to turn this essay into a jeremiad, because a jeremiad is a self-indulgently enjoyable thing to write and I am not, at the moment, writing to enjoy myself but to get certain matters into a clearer perspective. In any case, a jeremiad would be foolish. This is a good period of literature; it is the age of Neruda and Paz and Günter Grass and Moravia and Golding and Iris Murdoch and Larkin and R. S. Thomas and Leonardo Sciascia and dozens more, including that marvellous Latin American writer Gabriel Garcia Márquez who wrote *A Hundred Years of Solitude*; and though Pasternak is dead, Borges and Montale and Ezra Pound are still alive. And even North American literature, dominated as it is at the moment by the showmen and the brass-lunged shouters, will be heard to speak again when the deafening parade has gone by. Its voice will come from directions we have neglected, from the absolutely professional craftsmanship of a novelist like Alfred Hayes or the quiet, unstressed meaningfulness of a poet like David Wagoner. No, mere pessimism about 'the state of things', the writer's habitual snivel, would be out of place. What we need, those of us who enjoy the art of literature, whether as readers or writers, and wish to see it continue, is a sense of the importance of what is at stake and a quiet determination to face down the opposition. If imaginative writing goes, what remains? If language is never to be used for anything but information and analysis, if poetry, from being a repository of emotions and associations that would otherwise remain undefined and unfelt, becomes a play-area for delinquent children, how is a civilization possible?

The modern Puritanism of fact would imprison us in a strait-jacket of statement. And when poets retreat into the kindergarten and begin to turn out babble and doodle under such various earnest names as 'sound poetry' and 'concrete poetry', they are showing a flaccid willingness to cede the central territory they should be defending. Unreverberative factual statement on the one hand, play-patterns on the other, and in between only the crude slogans of the propagandists—is this what we want?

One thing that language can do better than any other form of communication is to liberate the individual by setting his imagination to work. If twenty people read the sentence, 'Autumn had come to the woods, and a thin white mist hung between the wet tree-trunks', twenty separate imaginative pictures will be formed. They will relate to a central core provided by the author, but they will be individual. And so on. In a novel, each reader imagines the physical appearance of the characters, hears the timbre of their voices, pictures to himself the physical setting of the action. In the cinema, by contrast, we all see what the camera puts in front of us. Only one imagination is at work—the director's. I used to quote with approval Cocteau's definition of a film as 'a dream that can be dreamed by many people at the same time'. I still think this is a good definition of film, but I no longer look on it with complacency: it seems to me, now, a dangerous thing for a crowd of people to dream their dreams in unison. Dangerous, because it ministers to that collective hypnosis in which a people, having long since lost touch with reality, is led to embrace ever more evil delusions. What, after all, was Fascism but a dream dreamed by a lot of people at the same time?—and those sleep-walkers proved expensive to wake up.

At this point, the modern academic steps in again, to remind me that my values are based on an obsolete regard for the individual. In an age of collectivism, here am I, quaintly, still making the unargued assumption that it is better for human beings to think and feel as individuals than as a mass. Haven't I realized (asks the modern academic, with a tolerant shake of his Arnoldian side-whiskers) that individualism was merely an episode in the history of human attitudes, that in any case it was never world-wide, being confined to the West and only there among relatively privileged people?—and that it arose from a purely fortuitous association between *laisser-faire* economics, small-scale means of production, and Christianity with its stress on the value of the individual soul? All of which have just about had their day?

I do, of course, realize all these things. But, while the factors that produced Western individualism may all be in decline, the individualism itself, having been called into being, may well outlast its causes. (It wouldn't be the first example of such a turn of events.) And the mere fact that the spirit of individualism, the assumption that the unique personality in each of us is valuable because of its uniqueness and not in spite of it, has found beautiful and memorable expression in literature, will surely act as a continuing force. One sees the concern for the individual in the process of coming into the European consciousness with Chaucer and Villon—to pinpoint two names merely representative—and, by the time we reach the epoch of Shakespeare, the individual has moved into the centre of the stage. All Shakespeare's plays, particularly the major tragedies on which his reputation mainly rests, are concerned with the clash between large-scale personalities, aflame with the incandescence of their uniqueness, and the vast impersonal universe to which, somehow or other, they must temper themselves. Indeed, Shakespeare's main service to the world may well have been that his plays dramatized, and so brought into full consciousness, the nature of the human conflict as it was to be during the centuries of individualism. If this is so, the lives of the gigantic individuals who act out Western history from the Renaissance to our own time were made possible by Shakespeare and the other writers who were nourished by him. Because large-scale individual characters had been imagined and portrayed and set talking and moving on a lighted stage, they were free to exist in 'real' life. And this, after all, is not more than the *cliché* that life imitates art; as one feels that Wilde and Pater were to a large extent creations of a movement in literature that began when they were children.

Western art, and particularly the art of literature, focused, defined, and in general gave a tremendous push to, the notion of the individual. And the cultural muddle of the present time is due, very largely, to the antagonism between the kind of art which keeps alive the spirit of individualism, drawing strength from it and channelling back strength in return, and the new collectivized art or anti-art which screens out the individual. And here we circle back to revolutionary Puritanism, because Asiatic peasants are too poor to know or care about individualism, and the Asiatic peasant is the kind of man we must all strive to resemble, because he is exploited and poor and holy and a Mass, and there is one thing needful. Or so the Puritans tell us, howling in the echo-chamber of a technological society.

We may be sure of one thing: the pushing and shoving will go on. The novel is an individual form, the film is not. Poetry which uses the full resources of its tradition is an individual form, though less so than the novel because the poetic use of language is always to some extent tribal; concrete-and-gimmick poetry is anti-individual because its means are too simplified to express the complexity of the individual nature; it is a means of togetherness. Narrative is individual because we all have our own way of telling a story; plotless, static mood-writing is anti-individual because it induces hypnosis, and the 'trip' is a shared experience if it is to be an experience at all.

The most easily available trip, if only because it costs nothing, does not involve the services of a pusher, and does not come into collision with the law, is of course the trip into one's own inner failures and miseries. To let down a bucket into the well of despair that we can all locate inside ourselves is not only easy and even, in its release from tension, rather pleasant; it is also a reliable clap-trap. George Orwell, in the essay 'Inside the

Whale', took a bearing on the self-indulgent hopelessness of so much of the minor literature of the 1920s:

Everyone with a safe £500 a year turned highbrow and began training himself in *taedium vitae.* It was an age of eagles and crumpets, facile despairs, backyard Hamlets, cheap return tickets to the end of the night. In some of the minor characteristic novels of the period, books like *Told by an Idiot*, the despair-of-life reaches a Turkish-bath atmosphere of self-pity.

Orwell, at any rate, can be cleared of the suspicion of being a hearty beer-swilling optimist refusing to face facts. It is he who remarked, almost as a parenthesis that needed no proof and no emphasis, 'A man who gives a good account of himself is probably lying, since any life when viewed from the inside is simply a series of defeats' ('Benefit of Clergy'). His own intimate knowledge of suffering and foreboding, the chaos at the heart of the individual experience, is as profound as Samuel Johnson's. Yet he does not, for that reason, issue the prescriptive criterion that has once again become fashionable in recent years: exhibit that chaos, in all its seething disorder and to the exclusion of everything else, if you want to be taken seriously!

People who lack the talent to produce art, yet want to get into the act in some way, nearly always try to legislate for it. There is always a lot of coaching from the touch-line, in the literary weeklies and such-like; all that changes is the nature of the advice, delivered loudly and with the threat of total failure and isolation at the back of it. Thirty years ago the writer was threatened with excommunication if he failed to show social responsibility and contemporary sensibility, which in effect meant writing about hydro-electric schemes from the correct class-angle. Today the shouting goes on but the orders have changed. The up-to-date critic now maintains that, since human life is cruel and ugly, therefore art must be cruel and ugly. A classic *non sequitur.* And also a prescription which would have narrowed the field of art intolerably ever since its first inception; human life has always, over vast areas and for vast numbers of people, been cruel and ugly, so that if these critics had existed from the beginning and had been able to impose their views, humanity would never have had any but cold, squalid, narrow, despairing art, in which case the human race would probably have died out by this time.

However, this school of critics has certainly imposed its views at present, as witness Ted Hughes's *Crow*, the most praised poem of the last five or six years. *Crow*, with its relentless probing of the depths of horror and violence, reads very much like a poem written expressly to appeal to the reigning critical *cénacle*; obviously Mr Hughes is too serious and too sincere a poet to write for this kind of motive, which makes the poem even more of a depressing example; it can only be that the incessant demand for horrors has got under his skin and produced this rash. Bad criticism is a joke, until it begins to spoil good artists, and then it becomes a crime.

Back in 1964—but how freshly it comes to mind today—the indispensable *Critical Quarterly* carried an interesting article by C. B. Cox and A. R. Jones, 'After the Tranquillized Fifties'. In it, the authors took approving note of the 'concern with violence and neurotic breakdown' which was beginning to be evident at that time in the work of writers as diverse as Robert Lowell, Sylvia Plath and James Baldwin. In the course of a lucid and skilful discussion of these tendencies—the exploration of intimate personal experience, the owning-up to anarchic impulses, the 'assumption that in a deranged world, a deranged response is the only possible reaction of the sensitive mind'—the authors note with apparent approval, or at any rate a total absence of expressed disapproval, such attitudes as that which they attribute to James Baldwin:

'To Baldwin, therefore, to live, to perceive reality, is to submit oneself to suffering and chaos. Breakdown, neurosis, even suicide, are a proper reaction to the human condition, for otherwise we are escaping from the truth.'

What Professors Cox and Jones here state calmly and dispassionately can easily become fuel for the superheated demand for more violence, more sickness, more perversity, with which we are now bombarded by the hopheads of the literary underworld. As I said, their article appeared in 1964. I must take some opportunity of asking these distinguished critics, for I know and respect both of them, whether, after the passing of nearly a decade, they are still quite so happy about it all. Certainly, in those days, they appeared very sure that wisdom lay in this descent into violence and perversity, rather than in the attempt at distancing and poise which they discerned in the English writing of the ('tranquillized') fifties:

> Many of the new writers of the 1950s had been young men during the last war. Their writing appears to stem from a denial of the horror of such facts as Dachau, Belsen and Hiroshima, a refusal to be contaminated by the chaos in which their youth had been involved. They withdrew from politics and fighting, and tried to celebrate the inviolate quality of their personal emotions in lucid, disciplined verse. Philip Larkin's recently published *The Whitsun Weddings* includes some of the best poems written in this mode, combining lucidity and compression of meaning with orthodox metres and rhyme. Larkin often makes the point that for him withdrawal from life is necessary for the preservation of the self, though in poems such as 'Dockery and Son', 'Self's the Man' and 'Send No Money' he explores with subtlety his own doubts and the heavy price he has had to pay. In the novel, Kingsley Amis and John Wain tried to return to the fictional modes of H. G. Wells and Arnold Bennett, to show the problems of man in society in a conventional manner, but in their fictions they withdraw from serious problems into farce. Both of them touch on problems of mental suffering such as suicide in Wain's *Living in the Present* or fear of death in Amis's *Take a Girl Like You*, but find it difficult to make an extensive study of such problems. Their humour comes from a deliberate refusal to be involved, a sense that life is so chaotic and irrational that farce is the only possible medium for its expression.

This is certainly a pertinent criticism; personally I would accept the implied limiting judgement on my very early work (the only book of mine actually mentioned here was published in 1955, since when I have consistently striven to deepen as well as broaden my area of attention). What worries me is the apparently bland acceptance that what we need in place of this 'deliberate refusal to be involved' (if that's what it is) is a plunge into sickness and hysteria. Are Professors Cox and Jones, in view of the flood-gates that have opened in the years since they wrote their article, still as happy about the love affair with disintegration and death?

The irrationality which overwhelms man comes, not from without but from within; the individual will, the urge towards order and stability, is in direct conflict with the anarchic depths of the individual subconsciousness. To *know thyself*, once the ideal of reason, is now a call to anarchy. Moreover, writers co-operating in their perversity with these forces, through drugs or homosexuality or what have you, ally themselves with the forces of irrationality in the belief that reality, happiness and truth lie in such an alliance. Nonetheless they all appear to assume that self-knowledge must bring man into conflict not only with his society and its mores but, more importantly, in conflict with his conscious self. Self-expression is no longer expression of the conscious but of the subconscious self. Thus in the war between the conscious and the subconscious mind the forces are heavily committed on the side of irrationality, violence, hatred and perversity.

The trouble is that this sacred quartet of qualities—'irrationality, violence, hatred and perversity'—can be faked as easily as any other qualities: much more easily, indeed, than wit or irony or compassion. The overwrought, hysterical tone which seems to be mandatory in present-day writing must be one of the easiest tones to reproduce mechanically; eighteenth-century poetic diction, by contrast, must have been at least as difficult as playing some game like whist. And *Crow*, in the end, won't prove as helpful a model as *The Dunciad*—which also has its climax of barely controlled terror, its vision of the cold, dark waters which lie under the thin ice of reason and tolerance.

There is an unmistakable panic, a powerful unfocused dread, behind Pope's vision of 'the sable throne' of 'Night primeval, and of Chaos old'. The Puritan with his all-or-nothing logic may assert that to express this panic in beautifully poised couplets and honed language is to be paradoxical. Yes. By such paradoxes, art lives.